The Rice COOKBOOK

The *Rice*
COOKBOOK

Anne Dettmer & Victoria Lloyd-Davies

The
Globe
Pequot
Press

OLD SAYBROOK, CONNECTICUT

As seasoning is a matter of personal taste, salt and pepper
have not been listed in the ingredients.

Library of Congress Cataloging-in-Publication Data.

Dettmer, Anne
  The rice cookbook / Anne Dettmer and Victoria Lloyd-Davies -- 1st
ed.
  p.   cm.
  Includes index.
  ISBN 1-56440-360-2
  1. Cookery (Rice) 2. Cookery, International. I. Lloyd-Davies, Victoria
II. Title.
TX809.R5L58 1993
641.6'318--dc20   93-32746
                                                                    CIP

Manufactured in Singapore
First American Edition/First Printing

CONTENTS

Authors' Introduction

Rice appears in an assortment of shapes and sizes, ranging from short and tubby, through gently rounded to long and slender. It is this vast array of different rice types and their individual characteristics that add interest and variety to our culinary experiences.

The Latin term for rice is *Oryza sativa*, a name used to describe a cereal that is thought to have, at the very least, 40,000 strains within its botanical family. Although it is not possible to cover each of these variants in this book, the rice types obtainable in today's supermarkets and specialty stores have been included.

Each rice type behaves differently when cooked, therefore choosing the correct rice when preparing a specific dish is essential to achieve the required result. Some people who imagine they lack the skill to cook rice may have inadvertently used the wrong rice. Once armed with the knowledge of marrying rice types to cooking characteristics, the most inexperienced cook can prepare rice dishes with the flair of an accomplished chef. To dispel any mystique surrounding cooking rice, a cooking chart has been included on page 14, but do remember the cooking times are only a guideline.

To explore the world of rice is an exciting journey. Grown on every continent of the world except Antarctica, rice has inspired some of the finest culinary creations from around the globe. You will find many of these dishes within this collection of recipes, such as the classic and elegant risottos of Italy, the robust and fiery American Cajun and Creole dishes, the skilfully spiced Middle Eastern and Southeast Asian recipes, the colorful creations of Spain and the precisely prepared delicacies of Japan. You will discover not only familiar dishes that you may have enjoyed in ethnic restaurants or while traveling, but also those which may surprise you by their novel and ingenious treatment of rice.

There are recipes to suit every occasion, whether formal or informal entertaining, quick suppers and family meals, snacks, appetizers, salads or desserts. Many of the recipes in this book are suitable for vegetarians. And, as all rice is gluten-free, coeliacs can safely eat it, so adding interest to a diet which must avoid products that contain the protein gluten.

One of the joys of rice is that rice is always on hand when you need it. Not restricted by seasonal availability, rice will keep in the kitchen cupboard for some time before its expiration date. This is an advantage if you wish to try a recipe using a rice type which is unfamiliar to you, as you will not have to worry about wasting part of the package, and you can try the rice again at a later date. With this in mind, it is worth experimenting with many varieties of rice. Remember too that there is no laborious peeling or preparation to be done and that most rice approximately trebles in size when cooked. This is particularly beneficial when storage space is at a premium, such as on camping trips. For these occasions, several of the one-pot and stir-fry recipes in this book would be ideal.

For those who need meals quickly, some recipes based on convenience rice, such as frozen rice, are included. These rices can make all the difference when time is tight and water in quantity is difficult to obtain. With its amazing versatility in recipes and in type, its healthy attributes and simplicity in cooking, rice is a truly splendid and special grain, and one to sample time and time again.

Victoria Lloyd-Davies

THE HISTORY OF RICE

To pin-point exactly when mankind first realized that the rice plant was a food source and began its cultivation is impossible. Many historians believe that it was grown as far back as 5000 years B.C.

Archaeologists excavating in India discovered rice that, they were convinced, could be dated to 4530 B.C. However, the first recorded mention originates from China in 2800 BC. The Chinese emperor, Shen Nung, realized the importance of rice to his people, and to honor the grain he established annual rice ceremonies to be held at sowing time, with the emperor scattering the first seeds. Most likely, similar ceremonies took place throughout China with local dignitaries deputizing for the emperor. Nowadays, the Chinese celebrate rice by specifically dedicating one of the days in the New Year festivities to it.

Although we can not identify China, India or Thailand as being the home of the rice plant (indeed it may have been native to all) we can be more certain of how rice was introduced to Europe and the Americas. For that we have to thank the traveler, whether explorer, soldier, merchant or pilgrim, who took with them seeds of the crops that grew in their home or in foreign lands.

Not all seeds could be transplanted successfully, however. Great Britain has never been able to cultivate rice due to adverse climatic conditions. The rice plant requires immense quantities of rainfall in its early days, followed by a long and uninterrupted season of hot, dry weather. For this reason, many farmers must find ways to either flood the fields or drain the water from them at crucial periods.

In the West, parts of America and certain regions of Europe, such as Italy and Spain, are able to provide the correct climate thereby giving rise to a thriving rice industry. Some historians believe that rice traveled to America in 1694 in a British ship bound for Madagascar. Blown off course into the safe harbor of Charleston, South Carolina, friendly colonists helped the crew repair their ships. To show his gratitude, the ships' captain, James Thurber, presented Henry Woodward with a quantity of rice seed.

Some years later, the British unfortunately blotted their copybook in relation to the rice industry they had probably initiated. During the Revolutionary War, the British occupied the Charleston area and sent home the entire quantity of harvested rice, failing to leave any seed for the following year's crop.

The American rice industry survived this set-back and cultivation continued, thanks to President Thomas Jefferson, who broke an Italian law by smuggling rice seed out of Italy during a diplomatic mission in the late 18th century. The rice industry then transplanted itself from the Carolinas to the southern states surrounding the Mississippi basin.

Rice is so fundamentally important to various cultures that it is often directly associated with prosperity, and much folklore and legend surrounds the grain. In many cultures and societies, rice is integrated directly into religious belief. In Japan rice enjoys the patronage of its own god, Inari, and in Indonesia its own goddess, the Dewie Srie.

Rice is also linked to fertility, and for this reason the custom of throwing rice at newly wedded couples exists. In India, rice is always the first food offered by a new bride to her husband, to ensure fertility in the marriage, and children are given rice as their first solid food, eminently sensible as it is one of the easiest foods to digest. And, according to Louisiana folklore, the test of a true Cajun is whether he can calculate the precise quantity of gravy needed to accompany a crop of rice growing in a field. How easy to see that from its early beginnings to the present day, rice continues to play an integral role in sustaining both the world's appetites and cultural traditions.

Only fairly recently have major supermarkets begun to sell a substantial range of different rice types. With several exceptions, those described in this book can be purchased alongside your regular shopping needs, although you may have to buy some of the more unusual rices in specialty stores.

The various types of rice behave differently when cooked mainly because of variations in the ratio of the starches amylose and amylopectin they contain. If amylopectin is predominant, as it is in short- and medium-grain rice, the grains have a greater tendency to cling together when cooked, whereas if amylopectin is low and amylose high, as in long-grain rice, each cooked rice grain is dry and fluffy and remains separate.

Grains are classified by their length, and, on the whole, the longer the grain in relation to its width the more separate the grains will remain on cooking. There are always exceptions, however, such as jasmine rice, so although length is a good general guide, it is worth reading the descriptions that follow before making a definitive judgement based on grain length.

Although the individual characteristics for each rice type govern their suitability for the preparation of specific dishes, there is one type that is labeled as long-grain and regarded by many as 'all-purpose'. Using long-grain rice for all dishes may indeed supply satisfactory results, but may not always conform to the ethnic correctness of the resulting dish. Nevertheless, knowing when long-grain rice can be substituted for a specialty variety is useful, so suggested substitutions have been included where appropriate throughout the book.

LONG-GRAIN OR ALL-PURPOSE RICE

The long-grains are exported mainly from the U.S., Italy, Spain, Surinam, Guyana and Thailand. At one time long-grain rice came from India and was called Patna after the district in which it grew. Long-grain rice has a slim grain that is four to five times as long as it is wide. Harvested straight from the field, long-grain is known as 'rough' or 'paddy' rice but undergoes different milling techniques to result in the following four choices.

REGULAR LONG-GRAIN WHITE RICE The husk and bran layers are removed in milling to produce a white grain. When cooked, the grain tends to separate and fluff, retaining a minute 'cling'. To avoid too much cling, ensure this rice is not over-cooked.

This rice has a subtle flavor that is complementary to either a richly flavored or delicate dish, so it is enormously versatile and can be used for numerous international dishes. This rice is ideal for American, Mexican, Spanish (except for paella) and Caribbean recipes and is particularly good for Chinese dishes, especially if chopsticks are to be used. Also try long-grain white rice for stuffings. Although it can be be used for Indian and Indonesian dishes, it would not be the correct ethnic choice.

REGULAR LONG-GRAIN BROWN RICE This type of long-grain undergoes only minor milling, sufficient to remove the husk, but leaving the bran layer intact. The flavor is distinctly nutty and the retention of the bran layer ensures higher fiber, vitamin and mineral content than is found in white rice. The grains remain separate when cooked, as with white rice, but they take longer to soften. The cooked grains will have a 'chewy' texture that many people enjoy. Long-grain brown rice can be used to prepare any of the dishes referred to previously, but is particularly suited to 'wholefood' styles of cooking.

PARBOILED LONG-GRAIN WHITE RICE Sometimes known as 'easy-cook', 'converted' or 'pre-fluffed', this type is the ideal choice for the novice rice cook. Unlike regular-milled long-grain white rice, which is milled direct from the field, parboiled long-grain rice is steamed under pressure first, while still intact, which hardens the grain making it virtually impossible to over-cook.

Regular Long-Grain White

Regular Long-Grain Brown

Parboiled Long-Grain White

Parboiled Long-Grain Brown

Another benefit is that the process captures much of the natural vitamin and mineral content present in the outer layers and pushes these vitamins and minerals into the grain itself, before the layers are discarded in the milling which follows. Although golden in color when raw, parboiled long-grain white rice turns white on cooking and the grains remain completely separate. It has a slightly fuller flavor than regular white rice but can be used in the same ways, although is not quite as good for Chinese dishes or stuffings. It is particularly suited to rice salads and stir-fries.

PARBOILED LONG-GRAIN BROWN RICE Ideal for both the novice cook and those who find regular brown rice slightly too chewy. Not only is it lighter than regular brown rice but it takes less time to cook. Again, parboiled long-grain brown rice suits wholefood and vegetarian dishes or anywhere its nutty taste will be appreciated.

SPECIALTY RICES

These rice types, from all over the world, include aromatics, risottos, waxy rice and pudding rice, among others, and they often have a specific ethnic use. Grown, cooked and eaten, more often than not, at the same location, these rices have been central to various geographical regions' survival, but now increased trade between countries has expanded availability and choice in many markets. Some countries, however, still consume all they grow. Improved farming practices may well yield new types appearing in the shops in the years to come.

THE AROMATICS The first class of rice that is termed 'specialty' is aromatic rice. This contains a natural ingredient known as 2-acetyl 1-pyroline, which is responsible for the fragrant taste and aroma. As with wines, the fragrance quality of aromatic rice can differ from one year's harvest to another. The finest aromatic rices are also 'aged' to bring out the aromatic strength.

Basmati White

Parboiled Basmati White

Basmati Brown

American Basmati White

Jasmine

American Jasmine White

American Jasmine Brown

Wild Pecan

American Popcorn White

American Popcorn Brown

Wehani

Risotto (Arborio)

Basmati Rice: This extremely slender, long-grain rice has a perfumed taste and aroma. Grown in India and Pakistan, mainly around the foothills of the Himalayas, it is used in Indian cuisine. Basmati white is the one most commonly served in Indian restaurants. The grains are separate and fluffy on cooking. The parboiled variety is a relatively recent introduction for those who appreciate the advantages of the easy-to-cook process. Basmati brown rice has a higher fiber content and even stronger aroma than basmati white.

Jasmine Rice: Also known as Thai fragrant rice, this rice originates from Thailand. Although the length and slimness of the grains suggest they remain separate on cooking, jasmine rice does become soft and slightly sticky when cooked. Its aroma is less pronounced than that of a basmati rice. It is used mainly in Southeast Asian cooking, but can also be used for Chinese dishes.

American Aromatics: The American rice industry has developed a series of aromatic rices with the fragrance of both basmati and jasmine rice. Available in either brown, white or mid-way between the two, called micromill, the grains are long-grain. There are several varieties, produced from an original strain known as Della. Some of the aromatics readily available are U.S. basmati and jasmine, Texmati, Jasmati, Wild Pecan and Popcorn. Another unusual aromatic is Wehani which is russet red in color. The American-grown basmati and jasmine brands can be substituted for Indian-grown basmati and Thai jasmine.

RISOTTO RICE Risotto is a category of rice that is used specifically to make the classic Italian risotto dish, and includes several types, such as Arborio and Carnaroli. Whereas most rices can absorb around three times their weight in liquid, a risotto rice has the ability to absorb up to five times. It is a medium-grain rice and during cooking starch is released, encouraging the grains to cling together. The perfect risotto recipe has grains that are creamy in texture but are just firm at the core. Italian risotto rices can often be bought at specialty stores. American-grown medium-grain rice can be used in the same way.

Risotto (Carnaroli)

Parboiled Risotto Brown

Bahia

Japanese Glutinous

BAHIA RICE A large short-grain rice originating from Spain, bahia rice is used to make the Spanish national dish - paella. Bahia is not available in the U.S., but American-grown short-grain rice or Italian risotto rice can be substituted for any recipe that calls for bahia.

GLUTINOUS AND WAXY RICE These types of rice are also known as 'sweet' or 'sticky' rice, and types available originate from Japan, China and Thailand. There is also a short-grain glutinous rice grown in the U.S., but which is not in common use for cooking.

Japanese Glutinous Rice: This rice has a round, pearl-like grain which becomes sticky on cooking and has a slightly sweet taste. It is used by Japanese cooks to make sushi, which is a mixture of rice, vinegar and sugar. The preparation can be laborious as the rice has to be fanned with a wooden paddle as it cools.

Chinese Glutinous Rice: Chalkier in color than Japanese glutinous rice, this rice is used mainly in the preparation of stuffings and for rice puddings.

Thai Glutinous (Waxy) Rice: This type is available in both white and black grains, both of which are popular for Thai desserts. It is not as round in shape as the Japanese and Chinese glutinous rice.

SHORT-GRAIN RICE Originally this type of rice was called Carolina rice due to its early source in America, but nowadays it is referred to as simply short-grain rice. There is also a short-grain rice imported from Italy, which may be referred to as 'pudding rice'. The grains, which are tubby and chalky white in color, stick together when cooked. Used mainly to make traditional rice puddings, short-grain rice is unsuitable for dishes where separate grains are desired. Both white and brown short-grain rices are available.

WILD RICE This is not actually a rice at all, but an aquatic grass that grows wild along the waterways of North America. Wild rice was the traditional food of American Indians who harvested it from their canoes. The plant would be hit with the paddle and if the grain was

Chinese Glutinous

Thai Black Glutinous (Waxy)

Short-Grain Rice

Wild Rice

ripe it would fall into the canoe. Any grain falling back into the water germinated to produce the next crop. Wild rice is very dark in color, ranging from brown to black, and the grain is extremely long. It is prized as a gourmet rice and can certainly be pricey. Many companies provide wild rice mixes, blending wild rice with either a long-grain or a basmati, to make a very attractive and more economical buy.

CONVENIENCE RICES

Cooking rice is neither laborious nor time-intensive, although there are days when shortcuts are highly desirable. To help with preparing meals quickly, it is well worth having commercially prepared rice in the kitchen cupboard or freezer. Be sure to read the cooking or heating instructions on the package before using.

FROZEN RICE Cooked and then frozen, this convenience rice is readily available in supermarket freezers. Packed in both multi-serving and single-portion packs, it suits either the microwave or conventional reheating. Frozen rice is normally ready to serve in around three minutes.

CANNED RICE Also ready-cooked, canned rice responds well to both microwave and conventional reheating, and is available in white and brown. Recent introductions include ethnic style mixes.

PRECOOKED RICE This rice has been cooked and dried, and, although not as instant as either frozen or canned rice, it is speedier to cook than a raw rice and it is normally ready in ten minutes. It is often available in portion-controlled packs.

BOIL-IN-THE-BAG RICE This rice is conveniently contained in portion packs so it is easy to calculate the required amounts. However, the cooking time is not reduced. Both brown and white varieties are available.

DRY RICE MIXES There is now a wide range of dry rice mixtures to choose from, spanning those which are lightly flavored with herbs and spices to those mixed with vegetables. Rice mixes are often packaged for

individual dinners, and they make a useful accompaniment to many meals. You can also add your choice of ingredients to make them a substantial meal in themselves.

RICE PRODUCTS

Rice can be milled to produce flakes, flour, bran and ground rice, which are used in baking, desserts and food manufacturing. Some well-known breakfast cereals are made with rice, and rice cakes are enormously popular. Suitable for sweet and savory toppings, rice cakes are very low in calories. A coeliac's diet can be supplemented by rice shapes to provide an alternative to wheat pasta, and rice bread and cookies can be purchased as well. Oriental rice noodles, edible rice paper and savory rice crackers are also widely available. Rice is also made into beer, wine, sake, vinegar and oil.

RICE NUTRITION

Rice is an extremely healthy food for a number of reasons. Rice is a complex carbohydrate, which means that it contains starch and fiber whereas a simple carbohydrate is a sugar. Simple carbohydrates are quickly digested and provide a fast energy boost, but one that is not sustained. Complex carbohydrates, however, are digested much more slowly, allowing the body to utilize the energy released over a longer period, which is nutritionally more efficient.

Rice has a very low sodium content and contains useful quantities of potassium, the B vitamins, thiamin and niacin. An average portion of rice (about $\frac{1}{4}$ cup uncooked) provides about 11% of the adult estimated average daily requirement of protein. One serving also has only 245 calories. Those looking to reduce their fat and cholesterol intake can turn to rice because it

LEFT: *Many rice products are available on the market, such as rice flakes, flour, bran, breakfast cereal, rice cakes and cookies, pasta and noodles, and vinegar, beer and sake.*

contains virtually no fat and no cholesterol. Rice is also gluten-free, so suitable for coeliacs, and it is easily digested, and therefore a wonderful food for the very young and the elderly. Rice is suitable for vegetarians and vegans, with brown rice in particular complementing vegetarian and vegan foods.

STORING RICE

Rice will keep for a considerable time, although it is wise to observe the expiration date shown on the package. Unopened packages of rice should be stored in a cool, dry cupboard, but once opened any unused rice should be transferred to an airtight container in order to keep out moisture.

Cool leftover cooked rice quickly, then cover it to prevent drying out or the absorption of smells and flavors from other foods, and either keep the rice in the refrigerator for up to 24 hours (providing the temperature is 40°F or below) or divide it into portions and freeze it. Follow freezer manufacturer's instruction manual for recommended storage times.

COOKING RICE

There are four main methods of cooking rice, and which to choose is a matter of personal choice. However, in some recipes, such as the Herbed Lemon Rice on page 40, a specific method should be followed. Please refer to the chart for quantities and times, and add salt to taste.

ABSORPTION In this method, a precise measure of cold liquid is added to a precise quantity of rice, so that by the end of cooking, when the rice is tender, all the liquid will have been absorbed. Put $1\frac{1}{4}$ cup of rice and the recommended amount of cold water into a saucepan. Bring to a boil and stir once. Lower the heat to a gentle simmer, cover the pan with a tight-fitting lid, and cook for the recommended time until the rice is tender and the liquid has been absorbed.

Rice Chart	Quantity of Rice for all methods	Quantity of Water for absorption method	Cooking times for all methods	Cooking times for Oven (350°F)	Microwave absorption method cooking times, plus 10 minutes standing. 650 watt Full Power
Regular long-grain white	1 1/4 cup	2 1/4 cups	12 minutes	40 minutes	8 minutes
Parboiled long-grain white	1 1/4 cup	2 1/2 cups	15 minutes	45 minutes	10 minutes
Basmati white	1 1/4 cup	2 cups	10 minutes	35 minutes	6 minutes
Parboiled basmati white	1 1/4 cup	2 3/4 cups	12 minutes	40 minutes	7 minutes
Regular long-grain brown	1 1/4 cup	2 3/4 cups	35 minutes	1 hour 15 minutes	25 minutes
Parboiled long-grain brown	1 1/4 cup	2 7/8 cups	30 minutes	1 hour 10 minutes	18 minutes
Basmati brown	1 1/4 cup	2 3/4 cups	25 minutes	50 minutes	16 minutes
Jasmine	1 1/4 cup	2 cups	10 minutes	35 minutes	6 minutes
Wild	1 1/4 cup	3 1/4 cups	45 minutes	1 hour 40 minutes	38 minutes
Medium-grain (risotto)	1 1/4 cup	1 quart	20 minutes	–	–
Glutinous/Waxy	1 1/4 cup	2 cups	15 minutes	–	–
Short-grain (pudding)	1/4 cup	2 3/4 cups (milk)	40 minutes	2 hours (300°F)	8 minutes + 40 minutes on defrost
Convenience rices	Check package instructions				

FREE SIMMER In this method the rice is added to a much larger volume of boiling liquid, then excess liquid is drained off at the end of the cooking time. Put 1¼ cup of rice and 1½ quarts of boiling water into a large saucepan. Bring back to a boil and simmer, uncovered, for the recommended time until the rice is tender. Drain in a sieve. Rinse with more boiling water. Drain and serve.

MICROWAVE This is a convenient method as the rice can be cooked and served in the same dish. However, the rice takes as long to cook as for other methods because it must have a 'standing' time of 10 minutes.

Put 1¼ cup of rice and the recommended amount of boiling water into a deep glass bowl or deep microwave container. Stir once. Cover and microwave on full power for the recommended time. Remove the bowl from the microwave and let stand for 10 minutes before serving - it will continue to cook and absorb any remaining liquid after you remove it from the microwave. You may need to reduce the liquid quantity by 3 tablespoons if you have a sealed container that reduces the evaporation of the liquid.

COMBINATION METHOD If you wish to cook rice before cooking the rest of the dish, cook rice either by the absorption or the free simmer until just tender. Cool in a sieve under cold running water. Drain thoroughly and refrigerate. When required, reheat rice in a covered glass bowl or microwave container on full power for approximately 4 minutes.

Alternatively, an electric rice cooker or rice steamer may be used. These are now widely available from several manufacturers and are particularly advantageous if you eat rice often or cook in large quantities.

REHEATING RICE

Rice can be reheated in many ways. Place rice in a covered colander over a saucepan of simmering water, and shake the pan frequently until the rice is hot throughout. Alternatively, rice can be added to a saucepan of boiling water, boiled for 2-3 minutes, then drained. Or, spread the rice in a well-greased baking pan, cover with foil, and place in a preheated oven at 375°F for about 30 minutes. Other options are to preheat a little oil in a skillet or wok and stir-fry the rice, or place the rice in a microwave-proof bowl with a little water and cook in the microwave for a few minutes until piping hot. Do ensure the rice is thoroughly heated.

HINTS AND TIPS

- Rice trebles in size when cooked. Allow about ¼ cup uncooked rice per person.

- Rinse rice to remove starch before cooking, not after cooking. It is not necessary to rinse any all-purpose long-grain rice, and never rinse or soak risotto rice.

- To rinse basmati, jasmine, glutinous and short-grain rice, place the dry rice in a deep bowl. Fill the bowl with cold water and swirl the rice around with your hand. Allow the grains to settle in the bottom of the bowl. Then carefully tip the bowl so the water drains out, leaving the grains. Repeat four to six times until the water runs clear.

- Soaking rice reduces its cooking time. To soak, place dry or rinsed rice into a deep bowl, fill it with cold water and leave for 30 minutes. Drain well through a sieve, then proceed as usual.

- As a general rule, use long-grain rice for savory dishes, medium-grain for risottos and short-grain for puddings and desserts. Regular milled long-grain rice is best for stuffings but use parboiled in stir-fries and salads when you want every grain to be separate.

- If you want separate grains, choose all-purpose long-grain or basmati rices. Risotto, jasmine and glutinous or waxy rices always cling together and should never be rinsed after cooking.

- Glutinous rice needs special care - always use a large saucepan and simmer at the lowest possible heat. Never lift the lid off the pan. Leave rice in the pan for 10 minutes after cooking.

- Always add boiling water or broth to rice when making a risotto or cooking in the microwave. If possible use homemade broths, such as vegetable water or liquid from simmered chicken bones.

- To cool rice quickly, put it in a sieve over a bowl, then gently prod, at intervals, with the handle of a wooden spoon. This will release steam and heat.

- For fried rice, cook the rice and refrigerate it for two hours before needed so that most of the moisture has evaporated. Then stir-fry in very hot oil to avoid the rice absorbing the fat.

- Always fill rice saucepans with cold water and leave them to soak while you eat to make washing them easier.

- Fluff up rice with a fork just before serving.

- Rice absorbs flavors, so cook it with meat, chicken and vegetable broths, fruit juices or milk. White rice also absorbs color from saffron, turmeric and curry spices.

- To settle upset stomachs, boil rice, without rinsing it first, then strain the starchy liquid into a jug. Allow to cool before drinking the rice water.

SOUPS & APPETIZERS

The use of rice is not confined to main courses and desserts; indeed, rice occurs in numerous guises to make soups and appetizers from around the world, one of the most unusual being lontong - small cubes of cooked, cooled rice, often used in recipes from the Far East.

RICE & CHEESE BALLS WITH TOMATO SAUCE

3 tablespoons UNSALTED BUTTER

2/3 cup BROWN MEDIUM-GRAIN RICE

1 3/4 cups VEGETABLE BROTH

3 tablespoons FLOUR

1 or 2 FRESH GREEN CHILIES, SEEDED AND FINELY CHOPPED

2 PINCHES BAKING SODA

1/2 cup GRATED CHEDDAR CHEESE

1/2 teaspoon MUSTARD POWDER

1 EGG, BEATEN

1/2 cup FRESH BROWN BREAD CRUMBS

Tomato Sauce

1 tablespoon OLIVE OIL

3 SHALLOTS, FINELY CHOPPED

6 TOMATOES, PEELED AND ROUGHLY CHOPPED

3 SUN-DRIED TOMATOES, FINELY CHOPPED

3 LARGE FRESH BASIL LEAVES, CHOPPED

Heat the butter in a saucepan. Add the rice and cook, stirring, for 2 minutes. Add the broth, bring to a boil and stir. Cover and simmer for 25 minutes until the liquid has been absorbed. Stir in the flour, chilies, baking soda, cheese and mustard. Cool.

Meanwhile, make the sauce. Heat the oil in a saucepan and sauté the shallots for 2 minutes. Add the fresh and dried tomatoes and simmer gently for 10 minutes. Stir in the basil, remove from the heat and cover.

Half-fill a deep heavy-based pan with oil and heat to 350°F. With floured hands, shape the mixture into 30 walnut-sized balls. Dip each ball in beaten egg, then coat in bread crumbs. Deep fry, six at a time, for 2 minutes until golden. Drain on paper towels. Reheat sauce gently and serve with the hot rice balls.   SERVES 6

CALIFORNIA COMPANY

1 1/4 cups LONG-GRAIN WHITE RICE

4 WHOLE CANNED PIMENTOS, CHOPPED

4 SMALL GREEN CHILLIES, SEEDED AND THINLY SLICED

6 LARGE EGGS

1/2 cup MILK

4 tablespoons GRATED CHEDDAR CHEESE

Preheat the oven to 350°F. Grease a 9 x 12-inch baking dish. Cook the rice as directed on page 14. Cool, then mix with the pimentos and chilies, reserving a little. Transfer to the dish. Whisk the eggs into the milk and pour over the rice. Sprinkle with the cheese. Decorate with pimentos and chilies. Bake for 35-40 minutes until set. Cool, then cut into squares.   MAKES 12

TOP: RICE & CHEESE BALLS   BOTTOM: CALIFORNIA COMPANY

ORIENTAL LETTUCE CUPS

1 ICEBERG LETTUCE

2 ounces LEAN PORK, COARSELY GROUND

2 ounces PEELED SHRIMP

1 teaspoon GRATED FRESH GINGER

1/2 teaspoon CORNSTARCH

2 tablespoons DRY SHERRY

1 tablespoon SOY SAUCE

1/4 cup LONG-GRAIN WHITE RICE

1 tablespoon PINE NUTS (PIÑONES)

1 tablespoon OIL

1/2 SMALL RED PEPPER, SEEDED AND CHOPPED

4 GREEN ONIONS, TRIMMED AND CHOPPED

7-ounce CAN WATER CHESTNUTS, DRAINED AND QUARTERED

1 tablespoon OYSTER SAUCE

Separate the lettuce leaves and arrange in twos or threes to make cup shapes. Put the pork and shrimp in a bowl and add the ginger, cornstarch, 2 teaspoons sherry and 1 teaspoon soy sauce and mix well together. Set aside.

Cook the rice as directed on page 14. Toast the pine nuts under the broiler until lightly browned.

Heat the oil in a wok or large skillet and stir-fry the pork and shrimp mixture for 2 minutes, until the pork is cooked through. Add the red pepper and green onions and continue stir-frying for a further 2 minutes. Add the pine nuts, water chestnuts, the remaining sherry and soy sauce, and the oyster sauce. Bring to a boil and cook for 1 minute. Spoon a little of the rice into the lettuce cups and top with the mixture. SERVES 4

DOLMADES

2 tablespoons OLIVE OIL

1 ONION, FINELY CHOPPED

1 CLOVE GARLIC, CRUSHED

1/2 cup LONG-GRAIN WHITE RICE

6 ounces GROUND PORK

3/4 cup WATER

24 FRESH GRAPE LEAVES

1 tablespoon LEMON JUICE

1/2 cup TOMATO JUICE

2/3 cup SOUR CREAM

Heat the oil and sauté the onion and garlic until tender. Add the rice and pork, and cook for 5 minutes. Pour on the water. Bring to a boil and stir. Lower the heat, cover, and simmer for 15 minutes, or until rice is tender and liquid has been absorbed. Transfer to a bowl and allow to cool. Preheat oven to 350°F.

Blanch the grape leaves in boiling, salted water for 1 minute. Drain on paper towels and lay dull-side upwards. Add the lemon juice to the rice mixture. Place a spoonful of rice mixture in the center of each grape leaf, fold, and roll up tightly. Pack tightly in an ovenproof dish, then pour the tomato juice over the mixture. Cover and bake for 45 minutes. Transfer tomato juice to a pan and boil to thicken slightly. Remove from the heat and stir in the sour cream. Pour the sauce around the warm stuffed leaves. MAKES 20-24

TOP: DOLMADES BOTTOM: ORIENTAL LETTUCE CUPS

ROLLED SUSHI

4 SHEETS OF DRIED NORI SEAWEED

Vinegared Rice

1/2 cup SUGAR

1/2 cup RICE WINE VINEGAR

1/2 teaspoon SALT

2 1/4 cups WAXY OR GLUTINOUS WHITE RICE

2 1/2 cups WATER

Filling

4 DRIED SHIITAKE MUSHROOMS, SOAKED IN HOT WATER FOR **30** MINUTES

2 tablespoons plus 2 teaspoons SOY SAUCE

1 tablespoon plus 1 teaspoon WATER

1 teaspoon OIL

1 LARGE EGG, BEATEN

1 teaspoon WASABI

2 ounces RAW FRESH SALMON FILLET, CUT INTO 1/4-INCH-THICK STRIPS

1/2 CUCUMBER, CUT INTO THIN STRIPS

To Serve

WASABI

SOY SAUCE

To prepare the rice, dissolve the sugar in the rice wine vinegar over a gentle heat. Add the salt then set aside. Wash the rice in several changes of water until the water is no longer milky. Leave the rice to drain for 1 hour. Put the rice and water in a saucepan. Cover the pan with foil, then a tight-fitting lid. Bring to a boil, then turn the heat to very low and cook for 20 minutes. Increase the heat to high for 3 seconds, then turn it off. Leave, covered, for 15 minutes. Do not remove the lid at any stage.

Empty the rice onto a large baking tray, then pour the vinegar mixture over it. Fan the rice with a rolled magazine or a pot lid, while mixing the rice gently with a dampened wooden spatula or spoon. Continue until the rice is at room temperature. Place the rice in a covered bowl and refrigerate.

Meanwhile, drain the mushrooms, discard the hard stems, then cut into thin strips. Cook the mushrooms over a gentle heat with 2 tablespoons of the soy sauce and 1 tablespoon of the water for 5 minutes.

Heat the oil in a small omelet pan or skillet. Beat the egg with the remaining water, then pour into the pan to cover the base evenly. Using a fork or spatula, lift the edges of the omelet, allowing the liquid to flow onto the pan. Continue until the omelet is nearly set. Remove from the pan and cool. Then roll up and cut into 1/4-inch strips. Cover and set aside. Mix the wasabi and remaining soy sauce together in a small dish.

Toast the nori, if necessary, by holding a sheet in a pair of tongs and waving it over a medium flame. The nori becomes paler in color and fragrant. Place one nori on a sudare (bamboo) mat or on a clean linen towel. Using a slightly wet hand, take one-quarter of the rice and spread evenly over the nori. Place one-quarter of the salmon strips along the center of the rice. Brush with a little of the wasabi mixture. Arrange one-quarter each of the cucumber, omelet and mushroom strips on top and to the side, in neat rows, keeping as close to the center as possible.

Moisten the nori edges with water. Using the sudare mat or towel to help, carefully roll up the sushi, keeping the filling in place with your fingers, if necessary. Cut into six equal parts using a very sharp, dampened knife. Repeat with the remaining ingredients. Serve the sushi cut-side up, with small bowls of soy sauce and wasabi.

MAKES 24

RIGHT: ROLLED SUSHI

SATAY WITH LONTONG

Lontong is an Indonesian recipe that constricts rice as it cooks so that the expanding grains form a mass that can be cut into squares. Traditionally, a banana leaf was used to make the container, but boil-in-the-bag rice is the ideal alternative. Lontong is always eaten cold. It should be cooked the previous day or allowed to cool for at least 6 hours before serving.

12 ounces LEAN PORK FILLET, THINLY SLICED
PEANUT SAUCE, SEE BELOW, TO SERVE

Lontong
1 SACHET BOIL-IN-THE-BAG LONG-GRAIN WHITE RICE

Marinade
1 tablespoon SOY SAUCE
1 CLOVE GARLIC, CRUSHED
pinch each of GROUND CORIANDER (CILANTRO) AND CHILI POWDER
1 tablespoon OIL
1/2 teaspoon GROUND GINGER
1 teaspoon BROWN SUGAR

Make the lontong first by lowering the rice into a saucepan of boiling salted water. Cover and simmer for 1¼ hours, checking the water level once or twice. Add more boiling water if necessary. Remove the bag of rice, which will be plumped up like a pillow, and leave to cool. Chill overnight. Cut the bag open and cube the rice.

To make the satay, mix the marinade ingredients together. Add the pork, cover, and leave to marinate for several hours in the refrigerator. Preheat the oven to 350°F.

Divide the pork equally between eight short bamboo skewers that have been soaked in cold water for 20-30 minutes. Place on a wire rack on a baking tray and cook in the oven for 20 minutes, turning once, until the pork is cooked through. Serve with lontong and peanut sauce. Also serve some raw vegetables in a bowl containing a little rice wine vinegar and water, if desired. SERVES 4

PEANUT SAUCE

5 tablespoons OIL
1/2 cup BLANCHED, UNSALTED PEANUTS
2 SHALLOTS, QUARTERED
1 CLOVE GARLIC
1 GREEN CHILI, SEEDED
1/8 teaspoon TERASI (SHRIMP PASTE) OR ANCHOVY PASTE
2 teaspoons TAMARIND OR LIME JUICE
1/2 teaspoon BROWN SUGAR
1 2/3 cups WATER
2 tablespoons CREAMED COCONUT, CHOPPED
juice of 1/2 LEMON

Heat 4 tablespoons of oil in a pan and sauté the peanuts gently for 3 minutes. Drain. Grind the shallots, garlic, chili and terasi finely in a food processor. Heat the remaining oil in a large skillet and sauté the shallot mixture for 1 minute. Add the tamarind or lime juice and sugar and cook for 1 minute. Add the water and bring to a boil, stirring.

Grind cooked peanuts finely in a food processor and stir into the pan. Simmer until the sauce thickens, stirring occasionally. Stir the creamed coconut into the peanut sauce and add lemon juice to taste. SERVES 4

RIGHT: SATAY WITH LONTONG AND PEANUT SAUCE

RISI E BISI

Risi e Bisi is a thick rice and pea soup, and the recipe originates from Venice. Serve as a substantial first course or as a light lunch with some warm crusty Italian bread.

4 tablespoons UNSALTED BUTTER

1 tablespoon OIL

1 ONION, FINELY CHOPPED

3 SLICES CANADIAN BACON, CHOPPED

2²/₃ cups SHELLED FRESH OR FROZEN PEAS

1¹/₄ cups MEDIUM-GRAIN RICE

6 cups HOT MEAT BROTH

4 tablespoons FRESHLY GRATED PARMESAN CHEESE

2 tablespoons FINELY CHOPPED CHOPPED PARSLEY

Heat half the butter with the oil in a large saucepan, and sauté the onion and bacon until tender. If using fresh peas, add to the onion together with 2 tablespoons broth, and cook for 5 minutes. Add the rice and cook, stirring, for 2 minutes. Pour on the hot broth. Bring to a boil. Cover and simmer for 15 to 20 minutes. If using frozen peas, add them after 10 minutes.

Stir in the remaining butter, the cheese and parsley. The mixture should resemble a very thick soup; add a little extra hot broth before stirring in the butter, cheese and parsley, if the soup is too much like a risotto.

SERVES 6

GUMBO

Gumbo is a Cajun dish for which there is no one definitive recipe. Some gumbos are thickened with okra, others with gumbo filé, which is ground sassafras leaves, but they always commence with a roux.

2 tablespoons BUTTER

1 tablespoon OIL

2 tablespoons ALL-PURPOSE FLOUR

3 ounces PORK BELLY, CHOPPED INTO SMALL PIECES

1 LARGE ONION, SLICED

2 STALKS CELERY, CHOPPED

4 cups SLICED FRESH OKRA, SLICED

14-ounce CAN PEELED TOMATOES

2 CLOVES GARLIC, CRUSHED

1 quart CHICKEN BROTH

1³/₄ cups LONG-GRAIN WHITE RICE

1 cup PEELED COOKED SHRIMP

1 pound COOKED CHICKEN, CHOPPED INTO SMALL PIECES

1 teaspoon FILÉ POWDER

1 teaspoon TABASCO

Heat the butter and oil in a saucepan. Stir in the flour and cook over a low heat, stirring to make a rich brown roux (be careful not to let it burn).

In a large saucepan, sauté the pork until golden-brown, add the onion and celery, and sauté for 5 minutes. Then stir in the okra and sauté for 3 more minutes. Add the tomatoes and their juice and the garlic, and simmer for 15 minutes.

Slowly pour the broth into the browned roux, stirring constantly. Bring to a boil, stirring, and simmer for 1 minute. Stir into the okra mixture. Cover and simmer for about 1 hour.

Meanwhile cook the rice as directed on page 14. Add the shrimp, chicken, filé powder and Tabasco to the gumbo 5 minutes before the end of cooking. Spoon into individual bowls and top with a scoop of hot cooked rice.

SERVES 6

TOP: RISI E BISI   BOTTOM: GUMBO

SALADS

Rice adapts well to cold salads, as it is simple to prepare in advance and reasonable in cost. Rice salads are perfect for serving large numbers of guests at barbecues, buffets or lunches. Molded salads are unusual and particularly appropriate for special occasions.

CHINESE CHICKEN SALAD WITH PEANUT DRESSING

1 1/2 *cups* COOKED LONG-GRAIN WHITE RICE

12 *ounces* COLD COOKED CHICKEN, SHREDDED

4 GREEN ONIONS, SLICED DIAGONALLY

1/2 *cup* SLICED BUTTON MUSHROOMS

1/4 *cup* BEAN SPROUTS, BLANCHED FOR 15 SECONDS

1/2 CUCUMBER, CUT INTO THIN STRIPS

Peanut Dressing

2 *tablespoons* CRUNCHY PEANUT BUTTER

1 SMALL CLOVE GARLIC, CRUSHED

2 *teaspoons* GRATED FRESH GINGER

1 *tablespoon each* LIGHT SOY SAUCE, WINE VINEGAR AND SESAME OIL

2 *tablespoons each* WATER AND FRESHLY CHOPPED CORIANDER (CILANTRO) OR PARSLEY

Cool the rice and combine with the remaining salad ingredients. Whisk the peanut dressing ingredients together until well blended, pour the dressing on the salad ingredients and stir well. Chill for 1 hour to allow the flavors to blend.

SERVES 4

HOT CHICKEN RICE SALAD

1 1/2 *pounds* COOKED CHICKEN, IN BITE-SIZE PIECES

3 *cups* COOKED LONG-GRAIN WHITE RICE

1 SMALL ONION, FINELY CHOPPED

1 WHOLE CANNED PIMENTO, CHOPPED

15-*ounce* CAN CREAM OF CHICKEN SOUP

15-*ounce* CAN CREAM OF CELERY SOUP

1/2 *cup* MAYONNAISE

4 STALKS CELERY, CHOPPED

3 *tablespoons* SLIVERED ALMONDS

1 *teaspoon* GARLIC SALT

4 *tablespoons* GRATED CHEDDAR CHEESE

1/2 *cup* RICE KRISPIES, CRUSHED

Preheat the oven to 350°F. Mix all the ingredients together, except the Rice Krispies. Transfer to a large buttered casserole dish. Sprinkle with the Rice Krispies and bake in the oven for 30 minutes until golden.

SERVES 8

RIGHT: CHINESE CHICKEN SALAD WITH PEANUT DRESSING

CALIFORNIA SUNSHINE RICE MOLD

1/2 cup PARBOILED LONG-GRAIN WHITE OR BROWN RICE

15-ounce CAN CRUSHED PINEAPPLE

5-ounce PACKAGE LEMON GELATIN

2 SMALL CARROTS, PEELED AND GRATED

2 tablespoons SEEDLESS RAISINS

2 ORANGES, PEELED AND SEGMENTED

2 tablespoons HALVED PECANS

LETTUCE

Cook the rice as directed on page 14. Drain the pineapple, reserving the juice. Make up the gelatin as directed on the package using the drained juice from the pineapple, plus water.

Pour half the gelatin into a 1-quart ring mold. Add the pineapple, carrots and raisins. Allow to set. Keep the remaining gelatin so it is just on the point of setting. Mix the remaining gelatin with the cooked rice and pour over the set gelatin. Chill in the refrigerator until set. Unmold and fill the center with the orange segments, pecans and lettuce. SERVES 6

TOSSED AVOCADO RICE SALAD

1 1/2 cups COOKED LONG-GRAIN WHITE OR BROWN RICE

grated zest of 1 LEMON

1 tablespoon TOASTED SUNFLOWER SEEDS

1 STALK CELERY, SLICED

1 cup CANNED RED KIDNEY BEANS, DRAINED

2 LARGE GREEN ONIONS, THINLY SLICED

1 LARGE RIPE AVOCADO

juice of 1/2 LEMON

2 tablespoons VINAIGRETTE DRESSING

Cool the rice and mix with the grated lemon zest. Place sunflower seeds, celery, kidney beans and green onions into a bowl. Peel, pit, and roughly chop the avocado. Add to the vegetables with the lemon juice and vinaigrette dressing, and mix well. Arrange a circle of rice on two plates, then fill the center with the avocado mixture. Serve immediately. SERVES 2

MELON & SHRIMP SALAD

18-ounce PACKAGE FROZEN PILAU RICE

1/2 SMALL CANTALOUPE MELON

1 tablespoon FINELY CHOPPED DILL

1 cup FRESH PEELED COOKED SHRIMP

1/2 BOSTON LETTUCE, WASHED AND TORN INTO SMALL PIECES

Cook the rice according to the directions on the package. Allow the rice to cool. Remove the seeds from the melon and cut the flesh into cubes or balls. Stir the melon into the rice with the dill and shrimp. Line a dish with lettuce and pile the rice mixture on top.

SERVES 4

TOP: CALIFORNIA SUNSHINE RICE MOLD BOTTOM: TOSSED AVOCADO RICE SALAD

THREE-RICE PARTY SALAD

This multicolored salad makes an attractive party dish for large numbers of guests. If desired, reheat the salad and serve warm for a buffet.

1½ *cups* WILD RICE

1½ *cups* LONG-GRAIN BROWN RICE

1½ *cups* LONG-GRAIN WHITE RICE

¼ *teaspoon* MUSTARD POWDER

juice of 1 LARGE LEMON

8 *tablespoons* WALNUT OIL

3 SHALLOTS, FINELY CHOPPED

4 *tablespoons* FINELY CHOPPED MIXED HERBS

Cook the three types of rice separately, as directed on page 14. When cooked, immediately spoon all the rices together into one large shallow dish to cool.

Whisk the mustard powder, lemon juice and walnut oil together. Stir into the rice with the shallots and herbs. Refrigerate for 2 hours to allow the flavors to blend. Serve cold. SERVES 18

CORONATION RICE SALAD

The blend of spiced mayonnaise and dressing is absorbed by the rice in this vegetarian salad, imparting a variety of flavors to the final dish. You can substitute parboiled long-grain white rice for the basmati rice in this recipe.

1⅔ *cups* PARBOILED BASMATI WHITE RICE

3¾ *cups* WATER

4 CARDAMOM PODS, CRUSHED

⅔ *cup* MAYONNAISE

⅔ *cup* LIGHT CREAM

2 *teaspoons* GARAM MASALA OR CURRY POWDER

15-*ounce* CAN PINEAPPLE SLICES, WITH JUICE

1 *cup* DRAINED AND CUBED TOFU

1 RED BELL PEPPER, SEEDED AND THINLY SLICED

1 GREEN BELL PEPPER, SEEDED AND THINLY SLICED

6 GREEN GRAPES, SEEDED AND HALVED

6 BLACK GRAPES, SEEDED AND HALVED

1 STARFRUIT (CARAMBOLA), SLICED VERTICALLY

4 *tablespoons* WALNUT OIL

1 *tablespoon* WINE VINEGAR

Put rice, water and cardamom pods into a large saucepan. Cook the rice as directed on page 14. Drain and cool.

Meanwhile blend together the mayonnaise, cream and garam masala or curry powder in a large bowl. Stir in 3 tablespoons pineapple juice and the tofu. Cut the pineapple slices into bite-sized pieces. Add the vegetables and fruit to the mayonnaise mixture. Mix together the oil and vinegar and stir into the cooled rice. Mix well and refrigerate until cold. Stir the mayonnaise mixture into the rice. Pile onto a large serving platter. SERVES 8, OR 10 FOR A BUFFET PARTY

TOP: THREE-RICE PARTY SALAD
BOTTOM: CORONATION RICE SALAD

CHIRA-SUSHI

2 tablespoons OIL

1 LARGE CARROT, CUT INTO THIN STRIPS

1 ONION, CHOPPED

1 STALK CELERY, SLICED

1/2 cup GREEN BEANS, CUT INTO 1-INCH LENGTHS

1/4 cup PEAS

4 SHIITAKE MUSHROOMS, SLICED

1/2 cup CANNED SLICED BAMBOO SHOOTS, DRAINED

1 tablespoon SOY SAUCE

1 teaspoon SUGAR

1/2 cup COOKED, PEELED SHRIMP

FINELY SLICED FRESH GINGER

Vinegared Rice

3 tablespoons SUGAR

4 tablespoons RICE WINE VINEGAR

1/2 teaspoon SALT

1 PIECE DRIED SEAWEED, OPTIONAL

2 cups WAXY OR GLUTINOUS WHITE RICE

2 cups WATER

Omelet

1 teaspoon OIL

1 LARGE EGG, BEATEN

1 teaspoon WATER

To prepare the rice, dissolve the sugar in the vinegar over a low heat, add salt, then set aside. Put the dried seaweed, if used, and the rice into a saucepan with the water. When the seaweed has dissolved, cook the rice as directed on page 14. Tip the rice onto a large baking pan, pour over the sweetened vinegar and fan the rice with a rolled magazine or pot lid, while mixing the rice gently with a dampened wooden spatula or spoon. Continue until the rice is at room temperature.

For the omelet, heat the oil in a small omelet pan or skillet. Beat the egg with the water, then pour into the pan to coat the base evenly. Using a spatula, lift the edges, allowing the liquid to flow onto the pan. Continue until nearly set. Cut the omelet into thin strips.

Heat the oil in a skillet and stir-fry the carrot, onion, celery and beans for 5 minutes. Then add the peas, mushrooms and bamboo shoots, and stir-fry for 2 minutes. Finally add the soy sauce and sugar. Heat through gently. Mix the vinegared rice with the cooled omelet, vegetables and shrimp. Arrange in a serving dish and garnish with ginger.　　SERVES 4

GADO-GADO

1/2 cup SHREDDED SAVOY CABBAGE

1/2 cup GREEN BEANS, CUT INTO 1/2-INCH LENGTHS

1 cup CAULIFLOWER FLOWERETS

1 cup each SLICED CARROTS AND BEAN SPROUTS

2 tablespoons GHEE OR CLARIFIED BUTTER

1 ONION, SLICED

1/2 CUCUMBER, SLICED

2 HARD-BOILED EGGS, QUARTERED

1 QUANTITY LONTONG AND PEANUT SAUCE, SEE PAGE 22

Steam the cabbage, beans, cauliflower, carrots and bean sprouts separately until tender, then cool. Heat the ghee or clarified butter in a skillet and sauté the onion until crisp; reserve. Arrange the lontong in the center of a large platter, and surround with the vegetables, cucumber and egg. Garnish the sauce with the sautéed onions and serve poured over the vegetables, or separately.　　SERVES 4

TOP: GADO-GADO　BOTTOM: CHIRA-SUSHI

FRUITY RICE SALAD

1 cup PARBOILED LONG-GRAIN WHITE RICE

1/2 cup VINAIGRETTE DRESSING

1 teaspoon GRATED ORANGE ZEST

2 teaspoons HONEY

2 teaspoons ORANGE JUICE

1/2 teaspoon GROUND GINGER

2 ORANGES, SEGMENTED

1/4 cup YELLOW RAISINS

1/4 cup GRAPES, HALVED AND SEEDED

1/2 PAPAYA, PEELED, SEEDED AND CHOPPED

1 MANGO, PEELED, PITTED AND CHOPPED

Cook the rice as directed on page 14. Cool. Whisk together the vinaigrette dressing, orange zest, honey, orange juice and ground ginger. Combine the cooled rice and all the fruit. Pour on the dressing and toss with a fork. Cover and refrigerate until required. Fluff up and serve.   SERVES 4

VEGETARIAN RICE SALAD

1/2 cup SLIVERED ALMONDS

14-ounce CAN ARTICHOKE HEARTS, DRAINED AND HALVED

1 1/2 cups COOKED LONG-GRAIN WHITE RICE

1 1/2 cups COOKED LONG-GRAIN BROWN RICE

2/3 cup MAYONNAISE

1-2 teaspoons GARAM MASALA OR CURRY POWDER

SHREDDED ICEBERG OR BOSTON LETTUCE, TO SERVE

Toast the almonds until golden-brown. Put the halved artichoke hearts and slivered almonds into a bowl. Add the rices. Blend together the mayonnaise and garam masala or curry powder and stir gently into the rice mixture. Serve on shredded lettuce.   SERVES 4

RIGHT: FRUITY RICE SALAD

SIDE DISHES

The following rice dishes are not substantial enough to serve as a complete meal, and are better suited alongside another dish. Many fish, beef and chicken recipes are perfect for serving with rice, or choose one of your favorite ethnic dishes.

RICE PILAF

Pilafs owe their origin to Eastern Europe rather than India, home of the pilau. They often include dried fruit and nuts.

4 tablespoons BUTTER
1 LARGE ONION, SLICED
1 CLOVE GARLIC, FINELY CHOPPED
1¼ cups PARBOILED LONG-GRAIN WHITE RICE
2½ cups CHICKEN BROTH
½ teaspoon GROUND TURMERIC
½ cup YELLOW RAISINS
1 LEMON
1 ORANGE
1 tablespoon OIL
½ cup CASHEW NUTS
½ cup BUTTON MUSHROOMS

Heat the butter in a large skillet and sauté the onion and garlic for 2 minutes. Stir in the rice and cook for 2 minutes. Add the broth, turmeric and raisins. Bring to a boil, stir, then lower the heat to simmer. Cover and cook for 15 minutes or until rice is tender and the liquid has been absorbed.

Cut thin strips of rind evenly from around the lemon and orange. Cut the lemon and orange into wedges. Blanch the lemon and orange strips in boiling water for a few minutes. Drain. Heat the oil and sauté the nuts until golden brown. Drain on paper towels. Sauté the mushrooms in the same oil until tender. Stir the nuts and mushrooms into the cooked rice. Serve garnished with the lemon and orange strips and wedges.

SERVES 4-6

FRIED RICE

1¼ cups LONG-GRAIN WHITE RICE
½ cup FRESH PEAS
2 tablespoons PEANUT OIL
2 ounces VIRGINIA OR PARMA HAM, CUT INTO THIN STRIPS
1 cup BEAN SPROUTS
2 LARGE EGGS, BEATEN
CHOPPED GREEN ONIONS, TO GARNISH

Cook the rice as directed on page 14. Cool completely. Cook the fresh peas until tender. Drain. Heat the oil in a wok or large skillet. Add the rice and stir-fry for 1 minute. Add the peas and ham and continue to stir-fry over a high heat for 5 minutes. Stir in the bean sprouts and the eggs and stir-fry until the egg is cooked. Transfer to a serving dish and garnish. SERVES 4-6

RIGHT: RICE PILAF

CHELO

This Persian dish is distinctive for its golden-crusted rice grains and is best served with sauces and meat dishes. The crust is called Tah e dig and considered a delicacy. A variation in which other ingredients are cooked with the rice is called Polo.

large pinch SAFFRON THREADS, CRUSHED
1 tablespoon HOT WATER
1¹/₂ cups PARBOILED LONG-GRAIN WHITE RICE
¹/₂ cup BUTTER

Soak the saffron in the hot water for 1 hour. Cook the rice as directed on page 14, but reduce the cooking time to 10 minutes when the rice is barely tender. Drain through a sieve and rinse under warm water. Drain well, making holes in the rice with the handle of a wooden spoon to release steam and heat.

Melt half the butter in a deep saucepan. Add 2 tablespoons of water and stir until hot. Add the cooked rice, and stir until the rice is well-coated, then build the rice up into a cone shape. Melt the remaining butter in a smaller saucepan, then pour the butter over the rice cone. Place a clean linen towel over the rice cone, and cover with a lid. Cook over a medium heat for 10 minutes, then reduce the heat to low and cook for 40 minutes. Do not remove the lid.

Spoon 3 tablespoons of the cooked rice into a bowl and mix with the saffron liquid. Spoon the remaining rice into a serving dish – the rice at the bottom of the pan should have a crisp brown crust. If it does not, turn up the heat for a few minutes. Add the saffron rice to the serving dish and mix gently. SERVES 4

SPICY BROWN RICE WITH VEGETABLES

2 tablespoons OIL
¹/₂ teaspoon CHILI POWDER
¹/₄ teaspoon GROUND TURMERIC
1¹/₂ cups LONG-GRAIN BROWN RICE
2³/₄ cups FRESH VEGETABLE BROTH
1 LEEK, SLICED
1 ZUCCHINI, THINLY SLICED
1¹/₂ cups SLICED BUTTON MUSHROOMS
1 cup VERY SMALL BROCCOLI FLOWERETS
¹/₄ cup PINE NUTS (PIÑONES)

Heat the oil in a saucepan and sauté the spices and rice for 4 minutes. Pour on the vegetable broth, bring to a boil and stir. Lower the heat, cover, and simmer for 20 minutes. Stir in the vegetables, cover, and continue to simmer gently for 10 minutes. Stir in the pine nuts. Cover and simmer for another 5 minutes.

SERVES 4

TOP: SPICY BROWN RICE WITH VEGETABLES
BOTTOM: CHELO

HERBED LEMON RICE

grated zest and juice of 1 LEMON
1¼ cups LONG-GRAIN, BASMATI OR JASMINE WHITE RICE
4 tablespoons FRESHLY CHOPPED MIXED HERBS, *or 2 tablespoons* DRIED MIXED HERBS
PARSLEY SPRIGS AND LEMON SLICES

Make up the lemon juice to the required amount of liquid with water. Pour into a saucepan. Add the lemon zest, rice and herbs. Cook by the absorption method as directed on pages 13 and 14, then garnish with parsley sprigs and lemon slices.

SERVES 4

SAFFRON RICE

½ teaspoon SAFFRON THREADS, CRUSHED
1 tablespoon HOT WATER OR BROTH
1¼ cups LONG-GRAIN, BASMATI OR JASMINE WHITE RICE

Soak the saffron in 1 tablespoon of hot water or broth for 1 hour. Put the rice into a saucepan. Add the saffron liquid, including the saffron threads, and the required amount of water. Cook by the absorption method as directed on pages 13 and 14.

SERVES 4

CURRIED RICE

2 tablespoons OIL
1 ONION, FINELY CHOPPED
1¼ cups LONG-GRAIN, BASMATI OR JASMINE WHITE RICE
1 tablespoon MILD OR HOT CURRY POWDER, SEE BELOW

Mild Curry Powder
1 tablespoon each GREEN PEPPERCORNS, CARDAMOM SEEDS, CLOVES AND CUMIN SEEDS
1 teaspoon each GROUND CINNAMON AND GRATED NUTMEG

Hot Curry Powder
1 tablespoon each GREEN PEPPERCORNS, CORIANDER SEEDS, GROUND TURMERIC
1-2 teaspoons DRIED CHILI FLAKES
1 teaspoon each GROUND GINGER AND CUMIN SEEDS

Heat the oil in a saucepan and sauté the onion for 2 minutes. Add the rice and curry powder and continue to cook, stirring, for 3 minutes. Add the required amount of water and cook by the absorption method as directed on pages 13 and 14.

Grind the spices to a powder in a spice- or coffee-grinder, or with a mortar and pestle. The blends can be altered to suit individual tastes. Store the remaining curry powder in separate airtight glass jars. Use within 1 month.

CLOCKWISE:
SAFFRON RICE, MILD CURRIED RICE,
HOT CURRIED RICE, HERBED LEMON RICE

DIRTY RICE

This Louisiana recipe is so-named because the chicken livers color the rice. It features the 'trinity,' which is the combination of celery, onion and green pepper used in many Cajun dishes.

2 *tablespoons* OIL

1 ONION, CHOPPED

2 STALKS CELERY, CHOPPED

1 SMALL GREEN BELL PEPPER, SEEDED AND CHOPPED

1 *cup* FINELY CHOPPED CHICKEN LIVERS

1 *teaspoon* CAYENNE PEPPER

$1^2/_3$ *cups* LONG-GRAIN WHITE RICE

2 *cups* HOT HOMEMADE CHICKEN BROTH

Heat the oil in a large saucepan and sauté the onion, celery and green bell pepper for 5 minutes. Add the chicken livers and stir well until browned. Stir in the cayenne pepper and the rice. Cook for 1 minute. Stir in the chicken broth. Bring to a boil. Cover and simmer for 12 minutes until rice is tender and the liquid has been absorbed.

SERVES 4-6

RED BEANS 'N' RICE

1 HAM HOCK

4 *cups* RED KIDNEY BEANS, SOAKED OVERNIGHT

$2^1/_2$ *quarts* WATER

1 *tablespoon* OIL

1 LARGE ONION, CHOPPED

2 STALKS CELERY, THINLY SLICED

3 CLOVES GARLIC, CRUSHED

2 BAY LEAVES

$1^1/_4$ *cups* LONG-GRAIN WHITE RICE

Simmer the ham hock in 3 cups of the water for 1 hour. Drain and reserve broth in a large measuring cup. Make up to 2 cups with water if necessary. Rinse the beans, put in a large saucepan with 2 quarts of the water, bring to a boil and boil for at least 10 minutes. Lower the heat and simmer for 1 hour until the beans are tender, adding more water as necessary. When cooked, drain and mash the beans a few times to give a creamy texture.

Heat the oil in a saucepan and sauté the onion, celery and garlic. Add the bay leaves and cook gently for 5 minutes. Add the rice and ham broth. Bring to a boil and stir. Lower heat, cover, and simmer for 15 minutes. Add the beans to the rice, and cook together for a further 5 minutes. Discard the bay leaves and fluff up the rice before serving.

SERVES 4-6

TOP: DIRTY RICE
BOTTOM: RED BEANS 'N' RICE

RISOTTOS

A classic Italian risotto demands undivided attention in cooking, because the skill is to add hot broth (which should be kept simmering) gradually during cooking. Time is well spent in producing the traditional risotto, but there are a few alternative methods given for those who require quick meals.

MILANESE RISOTTO

1 teaspoon CRUSHED SAFFRON THREADS
3 cups HOT CHICKEN BROTH
2 tablespoons BUTTER
2 tablespoons OLIVE OIL
2 CLOVES GARLIC, CRUSHED
1 LARGE BERMUDA ONION, CHOPPED
1¼ cups MEDIUM-GRAIN RICE
1¼ cups DRY WHITE WINE
3 tablespoons FRESHLY GRATED PARMESAN CHEESE
GENEROUS KNOB OF BUTTER
GRATED PARMESAN CHEESE, TO SERVE

Soak the saffron in the hot chicken broth for 1 hour. Heat the butter and the olive oil in a large saucepan. Add the garlic and onion, and sauté until soft. Add the rice and stir over a low heat for 2 minutes.

Add 1 cup chicken broth and simmer gently, stirring, until the liquid has been absorbed, then add another 1 cup of broth. Repeat as before, then add the white wine. When this has been absorbed, add the remaining broth and simmer gently, stirring, until the rice is creamy. Stir in the cheese. Add the knob of butter, stir, and serve with extra cheese.   SERVES 3-4

MUSHROOM RISOTTO

1 tablespoon DRIED MUSHROOMS
1¼ cups HOT WATER
3 tablespoons OLIVE OIL
1 ONION, FINELY CHOPPED
2 CLOVES GARLIC, CHOPPED
1½ cups MEDIUM-GRAIN RICE
2 cups SLICED BROWN-CAPPED BUTTON MUSHROOMS
2½ cups HOT FRESH VEGETABLE BROTH
1 tablespoon UNSALTED BUTTER
½ cup FRESHLY GRATED PARMESAN CHEESE
1 tablespoon FINELY CHOPPED PARSLEY

Soak the dried mushrooms in the hot water for 15 minutes. Heat the oil in a large saucepan and sauté the onion and garlic gently for 10 minutes. Add the rice and cook for 5 minutes. Strain the dried mushrooms, reserving the liquid. Add all the mushrooms to the pan and stir. Stir in 1¼ cup of the vegetable broth. Cook gently, stirring, until all the liquid has been absorbed. Add the remaining broth and repeat. Finally add the mushroom liquid and repeat. Stir in the butter and cheese, and garnish with parsley.   SERVES 4

TOP: MILANESE RISOTTO   BOTTOM: MUSHROOM RISOTTO

CERVELAT & PEPPER RISOTTO

2 tablespoons OIL

2 tablespoons BUTTER

1 ONION, CHOPPED

2 RED BELL PEPPERS, SEEDED AND CHOPPED

1¼ cups MEDIUM-GRAIN RICE

1 quart HOT CHICKEN BROTH

1 tablespoon TOMATO PASTE

3 tablespoons FINELY CHOPPED, FRESH PARSLEY

4 ounces CERVELAT SAUSAGE, CUT INTO STRIPS

1 pound CANNED PINTO BEANS, DRAINED

Heat the oil and butter in a large saucepan and sauté the onion and peppers for 2 minutes. Add rice and cook for 2 minutes. Stir in 1 cup of broth and simmer gently, stirring, until the liquid has been absorbed. Add another 1 cup of broth and repeat as before. Stir in the tomato paste, 2 tablespoons parsley, the cervelat, beans and another 1 cup broth.

Simmer gently, stirring, until the broth has been absorbed. Add the remaining broth and simmer until the rice is creamy. Serve sprinkled with the reserved parsley.

SERVES 4

MICROWAVE PEPPERONI RISOTTO

Risottos cook well in the microwave, and almost any recipe can be adapted to this cooking method. This method is based on a 650 watt microwave oven.

1 tablespoon OLIVE OIL

2 tablespoons BUTTER

1 ONION, CHOPPED

1½ cups MEDIUM-GRAIN RICE

4 cups HOT BEEF BROTH

¼ teaspoon TABASCO

7 ounces PEPPERONI, SKINNED AND SLICED INTO THIN STRIPS

16 STUFFED GREEN OLIVES

1 cup COOKED VEGETABLES, SUCH AS PEAS, CARROTS OR GREEN BEANS

Put the oil, butter and onion into a 2½-quart glass bowl. Cover and cook on full power in the microwave for 3 minutes. Add the rice and stir well until thoroughly mixed. Cover and cook on full power for 2 minutes. Add 1½ cups of the broth, and stir well. Cover and cook on full power for 5 minutes. Add another 1½ cups of broth. Cover again and cook on full power for 5 minutes. Stir in the remaining ingredients and broth. Cover and cook on full power for 10 minutes or until the rice is cooked and creamy. Let stand for 5 minutes before serving.

SERVES 4

RIGHT: CERVELAT & PEPPER RISOTTO

BROWN RICE VEGETABLE RISOTTO

2 *tablespoons* BUTTER

1 *tablespoon* OIL

1 ONION, CHOPPED

1 BULB FENNEL, CHOPPED

1 RED BELL PEPPER, SEEDED AND CHOPPED

1½ *cups* QUARTERED MUSHROOMS

1¼ *cups* LONG-GRAIN BROWN RICE

2¾ *cups* VEGETABLE BROTH

2 *tablespoons* FRESHLY GRATED PARMESAN CHEESE

1 *tablespoon* FRESHLY CHOPPED CORIANDER

Heat the butter and oil in a large saucepan. Sauté the onion and fennel for 3 minutes. Add the bell pepper and mushrooms and continue to cook, stirring, for 2 minutes. Add the rice, stir well, and cook for 1 minute. Add the broth, and bring to a boil. Stir once and lower the heat to simmer. Cover and cook very gently for 35 minutes until the rice is tender and the liquid has been absorbed. Remove from the heat and stir in the cheese and coriander.   SERVES 3-4

SMOKED FISH & MUSSEL RISOTTO

1 *tablespoon* OLIVE OIL

2 *tablespoons* BUTTER

1 ONION, CHOPPED

1 *teaspoon* GROUND TURMERIC

1 GREEN BELL PEPPER, SEEDED AND SLICED

1 YELLOW BELL PEPPER, SEEDED AND SLICED

1½ *cups* MEDIUM-GRAIN RICE

4 *cups* HOT VEGETABLE BROTH

1 *pound* SMOKED FISH FILLET, SKINNED AND CUT
INTO LARGE CUBES

2 *tablespoons* FINELY CHOPPED PARSLEY

1 *cup* COOKED, SHELLED MUSSELS

3 TOMATOES, PEELED AND CHOPPED

Heat the oil and butter in a large saucepan. Sauté the onion until soft, then stir in turmeric, green and yellow peppers and rice, and cook, stirring continuously, for 2 minutes. Stir in 1¼ cups of the broth and simmer gently, stirring occasionally, until the liquid has been absorbed. Add another 1¼ cups broth and repeat as before. Carefully stir in the smoked fish and parsley and another 1¼ cups broth.

Simmer gently, stirring occasionally, until the broth has been absorbed. Add the remaining broth and simmer until the rice is cooked and creamy. Stir in the mussels and tomatoes about 3 minutes before the end of cooking.   SERVES 4

TOP: BROWN RICE VEGETABLE RISOTTO
BOTTOM: SMOKED FISH & MUSSEL RISOTTO

CHICKEN LIVER RISOTTO

The wine in this classic recipe is boiled rapidly to give a wonderful flavor to the sliced chicken livers.

2 *tablespoons* BUTTER

2 *tablespoons* OIL

1 ONION, CHOPPED

1$\frac{1}{2}$ *cups* MEDIUM-GRAIN RICE

4 TOMATOES, SKINNED AND CHOPPED

8 CHICKEN LIVERS, SLICED

1$\frac{1}{4}$ *cups* WHITE WINE

3 *cups* HOT CHICKEN BROTH

4 *tablespoons* FRESHLY GRATED PARMESAN CHEESE

Heat the butter and oil in a large saucepan. Add the onion and cook for 1 minute. Add the rice and stir over a low heat for 2 minutes. Add the tomatoes and chicken livers and cook for 5 minutes. Pour in the wine and boil rapidly until the liquid has been absorbed. Add half the broth. Simmer, stirring, until the liquid has been absorbed. Repeat with half the remaining broth. Then add the remaining broth and simmer gently, stirring, until the rice is creamy. Stir in the cheese.

SERVES 4

CHICKEN RISOTTO

2 CHICKEN PORTIONS

2$\frac{1}{2}$ *cups* WATER

1 BAY LEAF

2 *tablespoons* UNSALTED BUTTER

1 *tablespoon* OIL

1 ONION, FINELY CHOPPED

1$\frac{1}{2}$ *cups* LONG-GRAIN WHITE RICE

2 *teaspoons* ITALIAN SEASONING

4 *tablespoons* FRESHLY GRATED PARMESAN CHEESE

1 *tablespoon* FINELY CHOPPED PARSLEY

Skin and bone the chicken portions, reserving the skin and bones. Cut the chicken into small pieces. Put the skin and bones into a saucepan with the water. Add the bay leaf. Bring to a boil. Cover and simmer for 30 minutes. Cool, then strain the chicken broth into a large measuring cup. Make up to 2$\frac{1}{2}$ cups, if necessary, with water.

Heat the butter and oil in a large saucepan. Sauté the onion and chicken for 3 minutes. Add the rice and Italian seasoning and cook for 2 minutes. Add the chicken broth. Bring to a boil. Stir once and lower the heat to simmer. Cover and cook very gently for 12 minutes until the rice is creamy and liquid has been absorbed. Remove from the heat, and stir in the cheese and parsley.

SERVES 4

LEFT: CHICKEN LIVER RISOTTO RIGHT: CHICKEN RISOTTO

STIR-FRIES

Stir-frying was originally created by the Chinese, but has become immensely popular all over the world. Using the stir-frying technique results in a dazzlingly fast meal. It is healthy too, as only a small amount of oil is used. Frozen rice, purchased from supermarkets, is convenient and ideal for stir-frying.

SWEET & SOUR VEGETABLE STIR-FRY

1¼ cups BASMATI WHITE OR BROWN RICE
2 tablespoons SUNFLOWER OIL
4 CARROTS, CUT INTO FINE STRIPS
1 ONION, SLICED
1 cup FRESH BABY EARS OF CORN
2 STALKS CELERY, CHOPPED
1 CHINESE CABBAGE (BOK CHOY), SLICED

Sauce
½ cup PINEAPPLE JUICE
1 tablespoon CORNSTARCH
2 tablespoons BROWN SUGAR
4 tablespoons WHITE WINE VINEGAR
2 tablespoons TOMATO KETCHUP

Cook rice as directed on page 14. To make the sauce, blend together the pineapple juice, cornstarch, brown sugar, vinegar and ketchup. Bring to a boil and stir until thickened. Remove from the heat, cover, and keep warm.

Heat the oil in a wok or large skillet until very hot but not smoking. Add the carrots, onion, corn and celery, and stir-fry for about 5 minutes until tender but crisp. Add the Chinese cabbage and continue to stir-fry for about 2 minutes until tender. Transfer the stir-fry to a bed of the hot cooked rice and pour on the sauce.

SERVES 4

ORIENTAL SEAFOOD STIR-FRY

2 tablespoons OIL
1 LARGE CARROT, SLICED DIAGONALLY
1 cup FRESH BABY EARS OF CORN
1 cup SNOW PEAS
8 ounces SHARK OR SWORDFISH STEAK, SKINNED AND CUT INTO STRIPS
2 tablespoons each SOY SAUCE AND HONEY
1 teaspoon GROUND GINGER
4 GREEN ONIONS, CUT INTO THIN STRIPS
14-ounce PACKAGE FROZEN THREE-GRAIN RICE OR OTHER FROZEN RICE

Heat the oil in a wok or large skillet until very hot but not smoking. Stir-fry the carrot, baby corn and snow peas for 2 minutes. Stir in the shark or swordfish strips and cook for a further 2 minutes. Add the soy sauce, honey and ground ginger, and cook for about 3 minutes, stirring occasionally. Stir in the green onions and frozen rice and cook over a moderate heat for 5 minutes.

SERVES 2

TOP: SWEET & SOUR VEGETABLE STIR-FRY
BOTTOM: ORIENTAL SEAFOOD STIR-FRY

CURRIED VEGETABLE STIR-FRY

1 tablespoon SUNFLOWER OIL
2 tablespoons CASHEW NUTS
2 tablespoons SUNFLOWER SEEDS
½ SMALL GREEN CABBAGE, SHREDDED
½ SMALL CAULIFLOWER, IN FLOWERETS
1 CLOVE GARLIC, CRUSHED
1 SMALL ONION, SLICED
½ teaspoon HOT CURRY POWDER
½ teaspoon GROUND TURMERIC
2 cups FROZEN YELLOW RICE
3 tablespoons HOT VEGETABLE BROTH

Heat half the oil in a wok or large skillet and sauté the nuts and seeds until golden-brown. Remove from the pan and drain on paper towels. Heat the remaining oil. Put the cabbage, cauliflower, garlic and onion into the wok and stir-fry for about 5 minutes, until the vegetables are tender but still crisp. Mix in the curry powder and turmeric and stir-fry for 2 minutes. Stir in the frozen rice and stir-fry for 5 minutes until thoroughly heated. Add the broth and cook a further 2 minutes. Add the nuts and sunflower seeds.   SERVES 2

SPICY LIVER STIR-FRY

2 tablespoons MILK
1 tablespoon TOMATO PASTE
1 teaspoon CHILI SAUCE
8 ounces LAMB'S OR CALF'S LIVER, CUT INTO THIN STRIPS
¼ cup PARBOILED LONG-GRAIN WHITE RICE
1 tablespoon OIL
4 CARROTS, CUT INTO MATCHSTICKS
1 cup GREEN BEANS
1 cup BEAN SPROUTS
½ cup CHICKEN BROTH

Mix the milk, tomato paste and chili sauce in a bowl, stir in the liver, and refrigerate for two hours to marinate. Cook the rice as directed on page 14. Heat the oil in a wok or skillet until very hot but not smoking, and stir-fry the carrots for 2 minutes. Add the beans and bean sprouts and stir-fry for a further 2 minutes. Add the liver, broth, and marinade, and cook for a further 4 minutes. Serve with the hot cooked rice.

SERVES 4

RIGHT: CURRIED VEGETABLE STIR-FRY

TURKEY STIR-FRY

Frozen rice and vegetables are excellent in stir-fries, providing an almost instant meal. Do ensure that the turkey breast is fully defrosted before cooking.

12 *ounces* FROZEN TURKEY BREAST, DEFROSTED AND THINLY SLICED

4 *tablespoons* SUNFLOWER OIL

1 *tablespoon* SESAME SEEDS

1 RED BELL PEPPER, SEEDED AND SLICED

4 GREEN ONIONS, CHOPPED

2 *cups* FROZEN BABY EARS OF CORN

1 *cup* FROZEN SNOW PEAS

1¹/₂ *pounds* FROZEN RICE, ANY VARIETY

Heat half the oil in a wok or large skillet until very hot but not smoking, and fry for 3-4 minutes, stirring continuously. Remove from the pan and keep warm. Pour the remaining oil into the wok and stir-fry the sesame seeds, red bell pepper and green onions for 2 minutes. Add the corn and snow peas, and stir-fry for a further 5 minutes. Return the turkey to the pan, add the frozen rice and stir-fry for 5 minutes until thoroughly heated. SERVES 4

THAI-STYLE RICE STIR-FRY

Long-grain rice can be substituted for jasmine rice in this recipe.

1¹/₂ *cups* JASMINE RICE

2 *cups* CHICKEN BROTH OR COCONUT MILK, SEE PAGE 68

3 *tablespoons* PEANUT OIL

2 CLOVES GARLIC, CRUSHED

2 GREEN ONIONS, CHOPPED

¹/₂ CUCUMBER, CUT INTO THIN STRIPS

1 *pound* FRESH GROUND LEAN PORK OR BEEF

2 GREEN ONIONS, SLICED

1-*inch* PIECE FRESH GINGER, PEELED AND GRATED

2 *tablespoons* LIGHT SOY SAUCE

2 *tablespoons* DRY SHERRY

1 *teaspoon* CHINESE CHILI OIL, OPTIONAL

1 *teaspoon* CORNSTARCH COMBINED WITH ²/₃ *cup* BROTH OR WATER

Cook the rice as directed on page 14 using broth or coconut milk (see page 68 for making up the coconut milk) instead of water. Cool. Heat 2 tablespoons oil in a wok or large skillet until very hot but not smoking, and stir-fry the rice. Add 1 crushed garlic clove, the chopped green onions and the cucumber. Stir-fry for about 4 minutes. Pile on a serving platter and keep warm.

Heat the remaining oil in the wok or skillet. Stir in the meat with the remaining garlic, sliced green onions and ginger. Stir-fry for about 5 minutes until browned and cooked. Mix in the soy sauce, sherry and chili oil, if using. Heat for 1 minute, then stir in the blended cornstarch and broth or water and stir until just thickened. Spoon on top of the rice. SERVES 4

RIGHT: TURKEY STIR-FRY

CHILI BEEF STIR-FRY

12 *ounces* RUMP OR FLANK STEAK, CUT INTO THIN
STRIPS

2 *tablespoons* PEANUT OIL

1 *cup* SLICED SMALL SUMMER SQUASH

1 *cup* SNOW PEAS, TOPPED AND TAILED

1 *cup* SLICED BROWN-CAPPED MUSHROOMS

1 *cup* BEAN SPROUTS, RINSED

1 *cup* COOKED STIR-FRY RICE OR
LONG-GRAIN RICE

juice of 1 ORANGE

Marinade

2 *teaspoons* SOY SAUCE

2 *teaspoons* RICE WINE OR SHERRY

1 *teaspoon* PEANUT OIL

$1/2$ *teaspoon* CHILI FLAKES

$1/2$ *teaspoon* GROUND FENUGREEK

grated zest of 1 ORANGE

Mix the marinade ingredients together in a large bowl. Stir in the sliced beef and marinate for 30 minutes. Heat the oil in a wok or large skillet until very hot but not smoking. Drain the beef, reserving the marinade. Add the beef to the wok and stir-fry for 2 minutes. Add the vegetables and stir-fry for 5 minutes. Stir in the rice, orange juice and reserved marinade, and stir-fry for 3 minutes.   SERVES 4

MICROWAVE TUNA STIR-FRY

Stir-fry recipes are successful in the microwave. Almost any recipe can be adapted to this cooking method. Always start with the harder ingredients first.

$2/3$ *cup* PARBOILED LONG-GRAIN WHITE RICE

1 *cup* BOILING WATER

1 *tablespoon* OLIVE OIL

4 GREEN ONIONS, CUT INTO 1-INCH LENGTHS

1 *cup* DRAINED AND SLICED BAMBOO SHOOTS

$1/2$ *cup* OYSTER MUSHROOMS, STALKS TRIMMED

$1/4$ *cup* BEAN SPROUTS, RINSED

3 CHINESE CABBAGE (BOK CHOY) LEAVES,
SLICED

1 *head* ARUGULA, SLICED

2 *cups* TUNA IN WATER, DRAINED

1 *tablespoon* OYSTER SAUCE

1 LIME

1 *tablespoon* CHOPPED TARRAGON

Put the rice and boiling water into a glass bowl. Cover and cook on full power for 6 minutes. Let stand for 10 minutes. Heat the oil in a large glass bowl on full power for 1 minute. Add the green onions and bamboo shoots. Stir well to coat in oil. Cover and cook on full power for 3 minutes. Stir in the mushrooms, bean sprouts, Chinese cabbage, arugula, tuna, oyster sauce, and grated zest and juice from half the lime. Cover and cook on full power for 3 minutes. Stir in the rice and chopped tarragon. Garnish with the remaining lime half, cut into wedges.   SERVES 4

TOP: MICROWAVE TUNA STIR-FRY
BOTTOM: CHILI BEEF STIR-FRY

STUFFINGS

Rice is as suitable as bread crumbs in making stuffings, and can help stretch expensive cuts of meat or fish. For a stuffing that is interesting in appearance and taste, and especially suitable for entertaining, try including a wild rice mixture.

GREEK STUFFED BELL PEPPERS

6 GREEN BELL PEPPERS

2 CLOVES GARLIC, FINELY CHOPPED

1 ONION, FINELY CHOPPED

1 tablespoon OIL

1 pound LEAN GROUND BEEF

$1/2$ cup LONG-GRAIN WHITE RICE

$1/3$ cup PINE NUTS (PIÑONES)

14-ounce CAN CHOPPED TOMATOES

2 tablespoons TOMATO PASTE

$1^1/4$ cups BEEF BROTH

2 tablespoons CHOPPED PARSLEY

2 tablespoons CHOPPED MINT

$1/2$ cup TOMATO JUICE

Preheat the oven to 350°F. Slice the tops from the peppers and discard the seeds. To make the filling, sauté the garlic and onion in the oil until softened. Add the meat and cook until browned. Stir in the rice and pine nuts. Drain the tomatoes, reserving the juice. Add the drained tomatoes, tomato paste, broth and herbs. Cover and simmer for 10 minutes. Fill the peppers loosely with the meat mixture. Stand the peppers in a shallow baking dish or pie-pan. Brush the peppers with oil. Mix together the tomato juices and pour around the peppers. Bake, uncovered, for 35-40 minutes.   SERVES 6

STUFFED TOMATOES

Long-grain rice can be substituted for medium-grain rice in this recipe.

4 LARGE TOMATOES

2 tablespoons OIL

1 SMALL ONION, FINELY CHOPPED

1 CLOVE GARLIC, CRUSHED

$3/4$ cup MEDIUM-GRAIN RICE

$1^1/4$ cups HOT VEGETABLE BROTH

2 tablespoons CHOPPED OREGANO

$1/4$ cup FETA OR GOAT'S CHEESE, CHOPPED

3 SUN-DRIED TOMATOES, FINELY CHOPPED

Preheat the oven to 350°F. Slice the tops off the tomatoes. Using a spoon, scoop out the pulp and seeds. Drain the tomatoes upside-down. Chop the pulp. Heat the oil in a large skillet and sauté the onion and garlic for 2 minutes. Add the rice and stir for 3 minutes. Pour in half the broth and cook, stirring, until the liquid has been absorbed. Add the pulp and remaining broth. Simmer gently. When the liquid has been absorbed, stir in the remaining ingredients. Fill the tomatoes loosely. Bake, uncovered, for 15 minutes.   SERVES 4

RIGHT: GREEK STUFFED BELL PEPPERS AND STUFFED TOMATOES

WHOLE SALMON WITH SPECIAL RICE STUFFING

Divide the stuffing ingredients in half for a 4-pound fish, and cook for about 45 minutes.

7-pound WHOLE SALMON
2 tablespoons BUTTER
1 SMALL ONION, FINELY CHOPPED
1/2 cup FINELY CHOPPED CELERY
1 1/2 cups LONG-GRAIN WHITE RICE
LONG STRIP OF LEMON ZEST
juice of 1 LEMON
1 teaspoon CHOPPED FRESH THYME
1 teaspoon CHOPPED FRESH BASIL
1 cup WATER
1/2 teaspoon GARLIC SALT
3/4 teaspoon FRESHLY-GROUND BLACK PEPPER
OIL FOR BRUSHING

Rinse the fish inside and out and pat dry. Remove the head and tail. Melt the butter in a saucepan. Add the onion and celery and sauté gently for 4 minutes, until the vegetables are soft. Add the rice and cook for 1 minute more. Add the lemon zest, lemon juice, water, herbs and seasonings. Bring to a boil. Stir once. Cover and simmer for about 15 minutes until liquid has been absorbed. Remove the lemon zest. Preheat the oven to 375°F.

Line a large baking dish with oiled foil. Lightly pack the stuffing into the fish and place the fish on the foil. Fold over the foil and seal by folding the ends in. Wrap any excess stuffing in foil. Bake the salmon for 75-90 minutes; add the foil package of stuffing for the last 10-15 minutes. Serve hot or cold. SERVES 14

WHOLE WHEAT PANCAKES WITH WILD RICE & SALMON FILLING

2 cups SKIM MILK
1 EGG, BEATEN
1 teaspoon SUNFLOWER OIL
1 cup WHOLE WHEAT FLOUR
1/2 cup ALL-PURPOSE FLOUR
LARD OR OIL FOR FRYING

Filling
2/3 cup LONG-GRAIN AND WILD RICE MIXTURE
1 cup FLAKED, COOKED FRESH SALMON
1 tablespoon FINELY CHOPPED, FRESH DILL
1 GREEN ONION, FINELY SLICED
2/3 cup CRÈME FRAÎCHE
1 tablespoon LEMON JUICE
SPRIG DILL, TO GARNISH

Cook the rice as directed on the packet. Meanwhile make the pancake batter by whisking the milk, egg and oil together. Add the flours and whisk until smooth. Set aside for 30 minutes. Mix together the salmon, dill, green onion, 4 tablespoons crème fraîche, lemon juice and rice.

To make the pancakes, heat a knob of lard in a skillet. Add about 2 tablespoons of the batter, swirl, and cook until lightly browned. Flip, and brown the other side. Make seven more.

Heat the filling gently. Fold the pancakes in quarters and spoon in the rice mixture. Serve garnished with the remaining crème fraîche and dill.

SERVES 8 AS AN APPETIZER, 4 AS A MAIN COURSE

TOP: WHOLE SALMON WITH SPECIAL RICE STUFFING
BOTTOM: WHOLE WHEAT PANCAKES WITH WILD RICE & SALMON FILLING

CAMPHOUSE TROUT WITH RICE STUFFING

4 TROUT, EACH WEIGHING ABOUT
10 OUNCES, CLEANED AND GUTTED
OIL FOR BRUSHING
LIME SLICES, TO GARNISH

Stuffing
3/4 cup LONG-GRAIN BROWN RICE
2 tablespoons PINE NUTS (PIÑONES)
1/2 cup SLICED BUTTON MUSHROOMS
1 teaspoon LEMON JUICE
PAPRIKA

Preheat the oven to 350°F. Cook the rice as directed on page 14. Cool. Mix the rice with the stuffing ingredients, adding paprika to taste. Divide most of the stuffing among the trout (any remaining can be heated and served with the trout) placing it in the cavity of each fish.

Place the trout in a roasting pan, brush with oil, and cover with foil. Bake for about 20 minutes, until the flesh flakes easily. Garnish with the lime slices, and serve with steamed asparagus, if desired. SERVES 4

COULIBIAKA

This Russian dish originally used buckwheat in place of rice. The traditional coulibiakas were very much larger than today's versions and had to be carried to the table by more than one person due to their size.

1/4 cup LONG-GRAIN WHITE OR BROWN RICE
2 tablespoons OIL
1 ONION, FINELY CHOPPED
1 LARGE CLOVE GARLIC, CRUSHED
grated zest of 1 LEMON
2 tablespoons FINELY CHOPPED, FRESH PARSLEY
1 tablespoon FINELY CHOPPED, FRESH DILL
1 pound SMOKED HADDOCK OR WHITEFISH FILLET, SKINNED AND CUBED
1-pound PACKAGE PUFF PASTRY DOUGH
3 LARGE EGGS, HARD-BOILED AND SLICED
BEATEN EGG OR MILK, TO GLAZE

Preheat the oven to 400°F. Cook the rice as directed on page 14. Heat the oil in a small skillet and sauté the onion and garlic until soft. Transfer to a basin and add the rice, lemon zest, herbs and smoked haddock or whitefish. Mix together gently.

Roll the dough out thinly into a large rectangle, then trim to 16 x 12 inches. Carefully lift the dough onto a baking tray. Spoon half the fish mixture onto one-half of the dough, leaving a narrow border around the outside edges. Cover with the sliced eggs, then spoon the remaining fish mixture over the top.

Make cuts 1 inch apart on the other side of the dough to within 1¼ inches of the three edges. Brush the edges of the dough with water, then fold the dough over the filling. Seal the edges well. Mark the dough with diagonal lines, then decorate with leaves cut from the dough trimmings. Brush with egg or milk, then bake for 30-35 minutes. SERVES 6

LEFT: COULIBIAKA
RIGHT: CAMPHOUSE TROUT WITH RICE STUFFING

CORNISH GAME HENS WITH PISTACHIOS & WILD RICE

2 *tablespoons* BASMATI RICE

2 *tablespoons* WILD RICE

4 *tablespoons* UNSALTED BUTTER

1 SMALL LEEK, TRIMMED AND SLICED

2 *tablespoons* SHELLED PISTACHIOS

grated zest of 1 ORANGE

2 CORNISH GAME HENS, EACH WEIGHING ABOUT 15 OUNCES

Preheat the oven to 375°F. Cook the rice as directed on page 14. Melt 1 tablespoon butter and sauté the leek until soft. Stir in the pistachios, orange zest and cooked rice, then mix well. Use some of the mixture to loosely stuff each bird. Place the game hens in a roasting pan. Dot each with the remaining butter, then roast for 50 minutes, basting occasionally. Reheat the remaining stuffing in a small saucepan and serve with the birds.

SERVES 2

STUFFED PORK CHOPS WITH ORANGE RICE

This stuffing is also suitable for turkey escalopes or boneless chicken breasts.

8 PORK CHOPS, ON THE BONE

OIL, FOR BRUSHING

Stuffing

1 *tablespoon* BUTTER

2 SHALLOTS, FINELY CHOPPED

1/2 *cup* LONG-GRAIN BROWN RICE

1 1/2 *cups* VEGETABLE BROTH

1 SMALL ORANGE

1/4 *cup* FINELY CHOPPED PITTED PRUNES

1/4 *cup* CHOPPED ROASTED HAZELNUTS

1 LARGE EGG, BEATEN

To make the stuffing, heat the butter in a saucepan and sauté the shallots for 2 minutes. Add the rice and cook, stirring, for 1 minute. Pour in the broth. Bring to a boil. Stir once, then cover and simmer gently for 35 minutes until the rice is tender and the liquid has been absorbed. Cool. Preheat the oven to 375°F, or preheat the broiler.

Meanwhile, grate the orange zest, remove the pith and chop the orange flesh into small pieces. Mix together the orange zest and flesh, the prunes, hazelnuts, cooled rice and the egg.

Trim the fat from each pork chop and use a sharp knife to slice the meat horizontally to make a pocket. Fill each cavity with the stuffing and secure with a skewer or string. Brush the chops with oil and bake for 20 minutes or broil for 15 minutes, turning once during cooking. Remove the skewers or string before serving.

SERVES 4-8

TOP: CORNISH GAME HENS WITH PISTACHIOS & WILD RICE
BOTTOM: STUFFED PORK CHOPS WITH ORANGE RICE

Main Dishes

Many acclaimed international dishes are accompanied by plain or lightly spiced rice, allowing the flavor of the main dish to be enhanced by the simplicity of the rice. Chicken Provençal, for example, is served with rice that has been flavored with just oregano and lemon.

Thai Chicken with Jasmine Rice

4 LARGE BONELESS, SKINNED CHICKEN THIGHS
2 tablespoons OIL
1 LARGE ONION, VERY FINELY CHOPPED
1 FRESH GREEN CHILI, FINELY CHOPPED
2 tablespoons each NAM PLA (FISH SAUCE) AND KETCHUP
juice of 1 LIME
1 STALK FRESH LEMONGRASS, SPLIT

Stuffing
8 ounces LEAN GROUND PORK
3 CLOVES GARLIC, CRUSHED
10 BLACK PEPPERCORNS, FRESHLY GROUND
grated zest of 1 LIME
2 tablespoons CHOPPED CORIANDER (CILANTRO)

Rice Mixture
4 tablespoons COCONUT MILK POWDER
1 1/2 cups JASMINE RICE

Mix all the ingredients for the stuffing together. Beat out the chicken with a steak hammer between sheets of nonstick baking paper until thin. Divide the stuffing among the chicken thighs, then roll up. Secure with string. Heat the oil and brown the chicken for about 10 minutes, turning frequently. Remove the chicken.

Sauté the onion and chili for about 3 minutes. Stir in the remaining ingredients. Replace the chicken, cover, and cook for about 30 minutes, turning occasionally.

For the rice, whisk the coconut milk powder into $1\frac{3}{4}$ cups water. Pour into a large saucepan. Add the rice. Bring to the boil, then stir once. Cover and simmer for 10 minutes until tender. Remove the string from the chicken and the lemongrass from the sauce. Slice and serve on a bed of the rice.   SERVES 4

Chicken Provençal

2 tablespoons OIL
1 LARGE ONION, SLICED
4 CHICKEN BREASTS, SKINNED
2 tablespoons each FLOUR AND TOMATO PASTE
14-ounce CAN CHOPPED TOMATOES
1/2 cup DRY WHITE WINE
1 CLOVE GARLIC, CRUSHED
2 tablespoons FINELY CHOPPED OREGANO
1 1/4 cups PARBOILED LONG-GRAIN WHITE RICE
peeled zest of 1 LEMON

Preheat the oven to 350°F. Heat the oil in a casserole dish. Add the onion and sauté for 3 minutes. Coat the chicken in the flour, add to the dish, cover, and cook until golden-brown. Mix together the tomatoes, tomato paste, wine, garlic and half the oregano. Pour over the chicken. Cover and bake for 30 minutes. Cook the rice as directed on page 14. Stir the remaining oregano and lemon zest into the rice.   SERVES 4

RIGHT: THAI CHICKEN WITH JASMINE RICE

LAMB VINDALOO WITH SPICED RICE

2 LARGE CLOVES GARLIC, CRUSHED

1 tablespoon GROUND GINGER

1 teaspoon each HOT CHILI POWDER, GROUND CORIANDER, (CILANTRO), CUMIN SEEDS AND GROUND CARDAMOM

1/2 teaspoon GROUND CLOVES

3-inch length CINNAMON STICK, LIGHTLY CRUSHED

2/3 cup RED WINE VINEGAR

2 1/4 pounds LEAN LAMB, CUBED

4 tablespoons GHEE OR CLARIFIED BUTTER, OR OIL

2 BAY LEAVES AND 12 PEPPERCORNS

Spiced Rice

2 tablespoons OIL

1/4 cup CASHEW NUTS

1 ONION, THINLY SLICED

1 CLOVE GARLIC, CRUSHED

1 1/2 cups BASMATI RICE

1 teaspoon each GARAM MASALA OR CURRY POWDER AND GRATED FRESH GINGER

a large pinch of CAYENNE PEPPER

about 3 3/4 cups HOT VEGETABLE BROTH

1 tablespoon FRESHLY CHOPPED CORIANDER (CILANTRO)

Put the garlic and spices into a bowl with the vinegar. Stir in the meat, cover, and leave to marinate in the refrigerator for about 24 hours.

Heat the ghee in a saucepan, toss in the meat, spices and vinegar with the bay leaves and peppercorns. Cover with a tight-fitting lid and simmer gently for about 1 hour. Remove the lid and simmer for a further 15 minutes to thicken the juices.

For the rice, heat the oil in a saucepan and brown the cashew nuts. Remove with a slotted spoon and reserve. Stir the onion into the pan and cook until just beginning to brown. Stir in the garlic, rice and spices, and continue cooking for 3 minutes, stirring. Stir in the hot broth. Cover and simmer for 10 minutes, until the rice is tender and the liquid has been absorbed. Stir in the nuts and sprinkle with coriander. Serve with the lamb.

SERVES 6

CHICKEN KORMA WITH BASMATI RICE

3 tablespoons GHEE OR CLARIFIED BUTTER

1 LARGE ONION, FINELY SLICED

1/2 teaspoon MILD CHILI POWDER

1/2 teaspoon GROUND TURMERIC

2 teaspoons GARAM MASALA OR CURRY POWDER

3/4 cup WATER

1-inch piece FRESH GINGER, SLICED

1 CLOVE GARLIC, SLICED

4 CHICKEN PORTIONS, HALVED AND SKINNED

2/3 cup PLAIN YOGURT

1/2 teaspoon each CUMIN AND CLOVES

1/4 teaspoon GROUND BLACK PEPPER

1 1/4 cups BASMATI WHITE RICE

Heat the ghee in a saucepan and sauté the onion until crisp. Reserve. Mix the chili, turmeric and garam masala with the water and pour into the pan. Bring to a boil. Simmer for 3 minutes. Add the ginger, garlic and chicken. Stir well, cover, and simmer for 20 minutes.

Turn the chicken over in the pan, then simmer, uncovered, for 30 minutes until the liquid has almost evaporated. Crush the crisp onion. Add the onion, yogurt and remaining spices. Simmer until the sauce is very thick. Cook the rice as directed on page 14, and serve with the chicken.

SERVES 4

TOP: CHICKEN KORMA BOTTOM: LAMB VINDALOO

FISH CREOLE

1¹/₂ *cups* LONG-GRAIN WHITE RICE

1 tablespoon OIL

1 CLOVE GARLIC, CRUSHED

1 LEEK, SLICED

1 GREEN BELL PEPPER, SEEDED AND SLICED

1-inch piece FRESH GINGER, PEELED AND FINELY CHOPPED

2 tablespoons GROUND CORIANDER SEED

1 teaspoon each GROUND CUMIN AND PAPRIKA

1 tablespoon ALL-PURPOSE FLOUR

2/3 cup FISH OR VEGETABLE BROTH

14-ounce CAN CHOPPED TOMATOES

1 BAY LEAF

1-1¹/₂ pounds COD, SCROD, PACIFIC RED SNAPPER, YELLOWTAIL OR PORGY FILLETS, SKINNED AND CUBED

8 STUFFED GREEN OLIVES, SLICED

1 tablespoon SUNFLOWER SEEDS

Cook the rice as directed on page 14. Meanwhile, heat the oil in a large saucepan and sauté the garlic, leek, green pepper and ginger for 5 minutes. Stir in the ground spices and flour, and cook for about 1 minute. Gradually stir in the broth and tomatoes. Bring to a boil, stirring until the sauce thickens. Add the bay leaf. Simmer, uncovered, for about 10 minutes. Add the fish and simmer for a further 7-10 minutes. Discard the bay leaf. Stir the olives and sunflower seeds into the cooked rice and serve with the fish.

SERVES 4

BOBOTIE

Bobotie is a South African dish consisting of an unusual curried meat mixture topped by a savory crust.

1¹/₂ pounds GROUND BEEF OR LAMB

1 ONION, CHOPPED

1 tablespoon MILD CURRY POWDER, SEE PAGE 40

1 teaspoon GROUND TURMERIC

grated zest and juice of ¹/₂ LEMON

14-ounce CAN CHOPPED TOMATOES

2 slices WHITE BREAD, CRUSTS REMOVED

1¹/₃ cups PART-SKIM MILK

2 tablespoons CHOPPED ALMONDS

2 tablespoons SEEDLESS RAISINS

1 tablespoon CHOPPED MANGO CHUTNEY OR SWEET PICKLES

2 LARGE EGGS

1 QUANTITY SAFFRON RICE, SEE PAGE 40

Preheat the oven to 350°F. Put the meat into a large saucepan. Heat gently to brown, stirring frequently. Stir in the onion and cook for 5 minutes. Stir in the curry powder, turmeric, lemon zest and juice, and tomatoes, and simmer gently for 15 minutes.

Meanwhile, soak the bread in 2 tablespoons of the milk. Stir the almonds, raisins and chutney into the meat. Squeeze the bread and tear into pieces. Add the bread to the meat and stir well. Transfer to a shallow 9 x 7-inch ovenproof casserole and cook in the oven for 30 minutes. Beat the remaining milk and the eggs together. Pour it over the meat and return to the oven for a further 30 minutes or until the egg mixture has set. Serve with the rice.

SERVES 4-6

RIGHT: FISH CREOLE

BEEF TERIYAKI

1¼ *pounds* STEAK, CUT INTO THIN STRIPS
1½ *cups* WAXY OR GLUTINOUS WHITE RICE

Marinade
6 *tablespoons* SOY SAUCE
2 *tablespoons* SWEET SHERRY
1 ONION, SLICED
2 *tablespoons* PEELED AND SLICED FRESH GINGER
1 *tablespoon* LEMON JUICE
2 *teaspoons* SUGAR

Mix the marinade ingredients in a large shallow dish. Add the meat and leave to marinate for 1 hour, turning the meat over once or twice. Cook the rice as directed on page 14. Meanwhile, preheat the broiler.

Remove the meat from the marinade and broil for 3-5 minutes, turning the meat once or twice and basting with the strained marinade. Spoon the hot rice into four oiled molds or cups and quickly invert onto four plates. Arrange the meat beside the rice and pour the warm juices from the broiler pan over it.   SERVES 4

GOULASH OVER RICE

2 *tablespoons* OIL
1¼ *pounds* LEAN PORK, TRIMMED AND CUBED
2 LARGE ONIONS, SLICED
4½ *cups* BEEF BROTH
3 *tablespoons* TOMATO PASTE
3-4 *teaspoons* PAPRIKA
2 *teaspoons* SUGAR
1 *tablespoon* UNBLEACHED FLOUR
1¼ *cups* LONG-GRAIN WHITE OR BROWN RICE
4 *tablespoons* SOUR CREAM

Heat the oil in a large saucepan and sauté the pork and onion until sealed on all sides. Add the broth and simmer for 10 minutes. Remove a little broth from the pan and blend with the tomato paste, paprika, sugar and flour until smooth. Stir into the pan. Bring to a boil, stirring. Cover and simmer for 1½ hours or until the meat is tender. Cook the rice as directed page 14. Just before serving, stir the sour cream into the meat and serve with the rice.   SERVES 4

CHILI CON CARNE

1 *pound* GROUND BEEF OR COARSELY-CHOPPED BEEF
1 LARGE ONION, CHOPPED
2 CLOVES GARLIC, CRUSHED
1 GREEN BELL PEPPER, SEEDED AND CHOPPED
1 *tablespoon* TOMATO PASTE
15-*ounce* CAN RED KIDNEY BEANS
14-*ounce* CAN CHOPPED TOMATOES
1-2 *teaspoons* HOT CHILI POWDER
1¼ *cups* LONG-GRAIN WHITE OR BROWN RICE

Put the meat into a large saucepan. Heat gently to brown, stirring frequently. Stir in the onion, garlic and green bell pepper and cook for 5 minutes, stirring. Stir in the tomato paste, kidney beans with their liquid, tomatoes with their juice and chili powder to taste. Bring slowly to a boil. Cover and simmer for 45 minutes. Meanwhile cook the rice as directed on page 14. Serve the chili con carne on the rice.   SERVES 4

RIGHT: BEEF TERIYAKI

One-Pot Meals

Most rice-growing countries have paid homage to their grain by devising a national dish. Generally cooked in one pot, the rice is mixed with other local ingredients. For example, in Cajun country in the U.S., crawfish and sausage are mixed with rice to make Jambalaya, and in Spain seafood is mixed with rice to create Paella.

Lamb & Tomato Pilaf

This recipe is a traditional dish from Eastern Europe in which all the ingredients are cooked together so the flavors will blend.

2 tablespoons OIL
1 LARGE ONION, CHOPPED
12 ounces LEAN LAMB, CUT INTO SMALL CUBES
1 CLOVE GARLIC, CRUSHED
6 TOMATOES, PEELED AND QUARTERED
2-3 BAY LEAVES
2 cups PARBOILED LONG-GRAIN BROWN RICE
CORIANDER (CILANTRO) AND LIME WEDGES, TO GARNISH

Heat the oil in a large saucepan and cook the onion and lamb over a gentle heat for 10 minutes. Stir in the garlic, cook for 15 seconds, then add the tomatoes and bay leaves. Cook for a further 10 minutes. Add the rice, cover with a tight-fitting lid, and cook over a gentle heat for 20 minutes. Discard the bay leaves, then garnish with coriander and lime.   Serves 4

Vegetable Pilau

Although a pilau is similar to a pilaf, a pilau is more highly spiced due to its Indian origins. You can substitute long-grain brown rice for the basmati rice in this recipe.

2 tablespoons OIL
1 LARGE LEEK, SLICED
1/2 RED BELL PEPPER, SEEDED AND DICED
4 STALKS CELERY, CHOPPED
1/2 teaspoon each GROUND CARDAMOM AND GROUND CINNAMON
1 teaspoon PAPRIKA
2/3 cup BASMATI BROWN RICE
about 2 cups VEGETABLE BROTH
2 SMALL HEADS OF BROCCOLI, IN FLOWERETS
1 SMALL CAULIFLOWER, IN FLOWERETS

Heat the oil in a large skillet and sauté the leek, red bell pepper and celery for 2 minutes. Stir in the spices and rice, then gradually stir in the broth. Bring to a boil, then add the broccoli and cauliflower. Cover, and simmer gently for 25 minutes, stirring occasionally, until the rice is tender and the liquid has been absorbed.   Serves 2

RIGHT: Lamb & Tomato Pilaf

CHICKEN BIRYANI

The Biryani originated in the north of India, and was served during festivals. The meat is steamed in a yogurt-based marinade. You can substitute parboiled long-grain white rice for basmati rice in this recipe.

1¼ *pounds* CHICKEN BREAST FILLET, CUBED

2 *tablespoons* GHEE OR CLARIFIED BUTTER

2 ONIONS, SLICED

1½ *cups* PARBOILED BASMATI WHITE RICE

3 BAY LEAVES

2 HARD-BOILED EGGS, EACH CUT INTO
6 WEDGES

2 *tablespoons* FINELY CHOPPED CORIANDER (CILANTRO)

Marinade

1¼ *cups* PLAIN YOGURT

1 *tablespoon* GRATED FRESH GINGER

2 LARGE BERMUDA ONIONS, CHOPPED

3 CLOVES GARLIC, CRUSHED

4-5 *teaspoons* HOT CURRY POWDER, SEE PAGE 40

Preheat oven to 375°F. Mix the ingredients for the marinade together. Stir in the chicken, cover, and leave in the refrigerator to marinate for at least 4 hours. Heat the ghee or clarified butter, then sauté the onions until golden. Lift out the onion and reserve a little for a garnish. Transfer the chicken with the marinade into a saucepan with the cooked onion.

Bring to a boil and cook, uncovered, over a low to medium heat for 15 minutes. Partly cook the rice in boiling water for 7 minutes. Drain. Place half the rice in a 2-quart casserole. Spoon the chicken and yogurt mixture over, then cover with the remaining rice. Gently press the rice into the liquid. Place the bay leaves on top. Cover with a tight-fitting lid and bake for 25 minutes until the rice is tender. Spoon onto a warm serving platter. Garnish with the reserved onion, eggs and chopped coriander.   SERVES 4

NASI GORENG

Nasi Goreng means fried rice and it can be served either as a meal in itself or alongside a selection of other Indonesian dishes. You can substitute long-grain rice for jasmine rice in this recipe.

1¼ *cups* CUPS JASMINE RICE

1 *tablespoon* BUTTER

2 LARGE EGGS

2 *teaspoons* WATER

2 *tablespoons* PEANUT OIL

4 SHALLOTS, SLICED

1-2 GREEN CHILIES, SEEDED AND SLICED

2 *cups* COOKED, DICED HAM

1 *cup* COOKED, SHELLED SHRIMP

1 *cup* COOKED, DICED MIXED VEGETABLES,
SUCH AS PEAS, CARROTS, CABBAGE

1 *teaspoon* SOY SAUCE

Cook the rice as directed on page 14, but do not allow it to become too soft. Cool and set aside for 2 hours.

Heat the butter in a 6-inch skillet. Beat the eggs with the water, then pour into the pan. Using a spatula, lift the edges of the omelet, allowing liquid to flow onto the pan. Continue until nearly set. Cut into strips.

Heat the oil in a wok or large skillet. Add the shallots and chilies and stir-fry for 1 minute. Add the ham, shrimp and vegetables and stir-fry for 3 minutes. Add the cooked rice and stir-fry until thoroughly heated. Stir in the soy sauce. Transfer to a serving platter and arrange omelet strips on top.   SERVES 3-4

RIGHT: CHICKEN BIRYANI

JAMBALAYA

Jambalaya is an infinitely adaptable dish traditionally made from leftovers and what was on hand. Cajun in origin, Jambalaya was a meal for the poor rural folk rather than their wealthier town cousins, the Creoles.

2 tablespoons OIL

4 CHICKEN PORTIONS, BONED AND CUT INTO CHUNKS

or 2 COOKED CRAWFISH

8 ounces CHORIZO SAUSAGE, CUT INTO CHUNKS

1 LARGE ONION, SLICED

3 STALKS CELERY, SLICED

1 CLOVE GARLIC, CRUSHED

1 GREEN BELL PEPPER, SEEDED AND SLICED

1 RED BELL PEPPER, SEEDED AND SLICED

6 cups CHICKEN BROTH

1¼ cups LONG-GRAIN WHITE RICE

½ teaspoon CAYENNE PEPPER

2 LARGE TOMATOES, SKINNED AND CHOPPED

Heat the oil in a large saucepan and brown the chicken. Add the sausage and cook with the chicken for a few minutes. Remove the chicken and sausage from the saucepan and keep warm.

Sauté the onion, celery, garlic and peppers until tender. Return the chicken and sausage to the pan. Add the broth. Simmer for 15 minutes. Add the rice, cayenne pepper and tomatoes, bring back to a boil, and stir once. Lower the heat to simmer, cover, and cook for 15 minutes, or until the rice is tender and the liquid has been absorbed. If using cooked crawfish, add to the pan for the last 10 minutes.   SERVES 4

KEDGEREE

During the days of the British Raj in India, it is believed that Kedgeree was adapted from Kichiri, an indigenous dish of rice and lentils.

2 tablespoons BUTTER

12 ounces SMOKED WHITEFISH OR COD, SKINNED AND CUBED

1¾ cups COOKED LONG-GRAIN WHITE RICE OR BASMATI WHITE RICE

1 tablespoon FRESHLY CHOPPED PARSLEY

1 HARD-BOILED EGG, CHOPPED

pinch of GRATED NUTMEG

grated zest and juice of ½ LEMON

Melt the butter in a large saucepan, add the fish and cook gently for about 5 minutes, stirring occasionally. Stir in the cooked rice and cook for a further 4-5 minutes. Add the parsley, egg, nutmeg and lemon juice. Cook, stirring, for a further 2 minutes, until piping hot. Garnish with the lemon zest and serve.   SERVES 4

RIGHT: JAMBALAYA

Paella

Paella originated in Spain and is the name of the oval, two-handled, metal pan in which this dish is cooked. Although recipes may vary, meat and fish are traditionally mixed in the ingredients.

large pinch of SAFFRON THREADS, CRUSHED
1/2 cup HOT WATER
2 tablespoons OIL
2 tablespoons BUTTER
1 pound CHICKEN BREAST FILLET, CUBED
1 LARGE ONION, CHOPPED
2 LARGE CLOVES GARLIC, CRUSHED
1 RED BELL PEPPER, SEEDED AND CHOPPED
1 GREEN BELL PEPPER, SEEDED AND CHOPPED
2 1/2 cups MEDIUM-GRAIN RICE
2 cups DRY WHITE WINE
2 tablespoons FINELY CHOPPED PARSLEY
2 LARGE BAY LEAVES
about 1 quart HOT FISH BROTH
1 1/2 pounds COOKED MIXED SHELLFISH, SUCH AS
SCALLOPS, SQUID, SHRIMP AND MUSSELS

Soak the saffron in the hot water for 1 hour. Heat the oil and butter in a paella pan or very large skillet. Cook the chicken for 5 minutes until brown, remove, and keep warm. Sauté the onion and garlic in the remaining fat until tender. Add the peppers and rice, and cook for 2 minutes, stirring continuously. Stir in the saffron liquid, wine, parsley and bay leaves.

Simmer gently, stirring occasionally, until the liquid has been absorbed. Return the chicken to the pan with about 1 cup of broth and cook as before. Add about 1 cup of broth, stirring occasionally. Stir in the remaining ingredients and the remaining broth, and simmer gently until the liquid has been absorbed and the rice is creamy.   SERVES 8

Arroz con Pollo

Rice with chicken is thought to owe its birth to either Portugal or Spain. Simpler than a paella, it nevertheless provides a substantial all-in-one complete meal.

4 CHICKEN PORTIONS
1 tablespoon OLIVE OIL
4 teaspoons PAPRIKA
1/2 cup WATER
1 1/4 cups CHICKEN BROTH
1 1/4 cups PARBOILED LONG-GRAIN WHITE RICE
1 ONION, CHOPPED
1 GREEN BELL PEPPER, SEEDED AND CHOPPED
1 GREEN CHILI, SEEDED AND CHOPPED
14-ounce CAN CHOPPED TOMATOES

Preheat the oven to 425°F. Brush the chicken skin with oil and rub in the paprika. Pour the water into a large casserole dish. Put the chicken, skin-side up, in the casserole. Bake in the oven, uncovered, for 20 minutes. Remove the chicken from the casserole and keep warm. Lower the temperature to 375°F.

Pour the broth into the casserole, add the rice, onion, green bell pepper, chili and canned tomatoes. Stir well. Arrange the chicken on top of the rice mixture. Cover tightly and cook for 45 minutes until the rice is tender and the liquid has been absorbed.   SERVES 4

TOP: ARROZ CON POLLO   BOTTOM: PAELLA

Chicken Simmered with Rice & Lentils

Long-grain brown rice can be substituted for basmati rice in this recipe.

1 tablespoon OIL
3-inch CINNAMON STICK
3/4 teaspoon CUMIN SEEDS
6 CLOVES
3 tablespoons GHEE OR CLARIFIED BUTTER
1 ONION, SLICED
12 ounces CHICKEN BREAST FILLET, CUBED
2 cups BASMATI BROWN RICE
1 quart HOT CHICKEN BROTH
1/2 cup RED LENTILS
1 teaspoon GROUND CARDAMOM
1/2 cup RAISINS
1/2 cup TOASTED ALMONDS
2 tablespoons CHOPPED FRESH CORIANDER (CILANTRO)

Heat the oil in a large saucepan and sauté the whole spices for 2 minutes over a low heat. Add the ghee or butter and the onion, then sauté until the onion is golden. Stir in the chicken and cook for about 3 minutes. Stir in the rice and cook for another 5 minutes.

Increase the heat and stir in the broth, lentils and cardamom. Bring to a boil, cover, and simmer gently for 20 minutes. Stir in the raisins and almonds, cover again, and cook for a further 5 minutes, or until the liquid has been absorbed and the rice is tender. Stir in the coriander.

SERVES 4

Rice à la Valencia

Spain claimed the Philippines in 1521, and this dish, although inherently Spanish, is enhanced with a touch of the exotic in the form of coconut milk. Rice à la Valencia is served on large platters during Filipino festivals.

1/2 cup BUTTER
6 CHICKEN PORTIONS, SKINNED
8 ounces DICED LEAN PORK
1 ONION, SLICED
2 CLOVES GARLIC, CRUSHED
3 LARGE TOMATOES, PEELED AND CHOPPED
2 ounces SLICED GARLIC SAUSAGE
2 tablespoons COCONUT MILK POWDER
2 cups WARM WATER
2 cups LONG-GRAIN WHITE RICE
1 cup FROZEN PEAS
2 tablespoons PITTED, SLICED GREEN OLIVES
2 HARD-BOILED EGGS, QUARTERED
1 PIMENTO, CUT INTO STRIPS

Heat half the butter in a large pan and sauté the chicken until brown, for about 10 minutes. Remove from the pan and keep warm. Brown the pork in the butter. Remove from the pan and keep warm. Add the remaining butter to the pan and sauté the onion, garlic, tomatoes and garlic sausage for 5 minutes. Return the chicken and pork to the pan. Cover and simmer for 15 minutes.

Whisk the coconut milk powder into the warm water. Add the rice to the pan and stir in the coconut milk. Bring to a boil. Cover and simmer very gently for 10 minutes. Stir in the peas and olives and cook for a further 5 minutes, or until the rice is tender and liquid has been absorbed. Garnish with the eggs and pimento.

SERVES 6

RIGHT: Chicken Simmered with Rice & Lentils

PUDDINGS & DESSERTS

Virtually every country has its own version of rice pudding, from plainly prepared recipes to elaborate concoctions. The basic ingredients are rice, milk and sugar, but often fruit is added. Also included in this chapter are more unusual rice desserts and treats, such as Calas Tous Chauds, which are rice fritters served with a sauce.

TRADITIONAL ENGLISH RICE PUDDING

2 1/2 cups MILK
1 VANILLA BEAN
1/2 cup SHORT-GRAIN RICE
1 tablespoon SUGAR
1 tablespoon UNSALTED BUTTER

Preheat the oven to 300°F. Butter a 4-cup baking dish. Heat the milk slowly over a low heat with the vanilla bean until hand-hot. Cover and leave for 1 hour to allow the vanilla to flavor the milk. Put the rice into the buttered dish with the sugar and butter. Strain the milk over the rice and stir well. Bake, uncovered, for 2 hours, stirring in the first two skins that form, then allowing the pudding to finish cooking undisturbed.

SERVES 4

SOUTHERN RICE PUDDING

This American version of the recipe above reflects a Mexican influence. A similar pudding is popular with the Portuguese who often add generous quantities of dried fruit, nuts and spices.

1 cup WATER
1/3 cup SHORT-GRAIN RICE
1 VANILLA BEAN
pinch of SALT
2 1/2 cups MILK
2 LARGE EGGS, BEATEN
3 tablespoons SUGAR
1/4 teaspoon GROUND CINNAMON
3 tablespoons SEEDLESS RAISINS
FRESHLY GRATED NUTMEG

Preheat the oven to 350°F. Butter a 6-cup deep pie plate. Bring the water to the boil in a saucepan. Add the rice, vanilla bean and salt and simmer very gently for 10 minutes, until all the liquid has been absorbed. Pour in half the milk and simmer for another 10 minutes.

Meanwhile, beat together the remaining milk, eggs, sugar and cinnamon. Remove the pan from the heat and stir in the egg mixture. Remove the vanilla bean. Pour the rice mixture in to the buttered pie plate. Stir in the raisins and sprinkle with nutmeg. Stand the pie plate in a roasting pan half-filled with hot water. Bake, uncovered, for 1 hour until the pudding is firm. Serve hot or cold.

SERVES 6

TOP: TRADITIONAL ENGLISH RICE PUDDING   BOTTOM: SOUTHERN RICE PUDDING

RASPBERRY BRÛLÉE

1/2 cup RICE FLOUR
2 tablespoons SUGAR
1/2 teaspoon GROUND CINNAMON
2 1/2 cups MILK
1 1/2 cups FRESH RASPBERRIES
6 tablespoons LIGHT BROWN SUGAR

Put the rice flour, sugar and cinnamon in a saucepan and gradually stir in the milk. Bring to a boil, stirring. Reduce the heat to very low and cook for 10 minutes, stirring frequently. Carefully stir in the raspberries, then transfer to a 8 x 6-inch ovenproof dish or six individual molds. Preheat the broiler to very hot. Sprinkle the brown sugar over the rice to completely cover the surface. Place under the broiler until the sugar caramelizes. Serve immediately. SERVES 6

PEACH MERINGUE DESSERT

1/2 cup SHORT-GRAIN RICE
2 1/2 cups MILK
5 tablespoons SUGAR
1/2 teaspoon FRESHLY GRATED NUTMEG
2 LARGE EGGS, SEPARATED
3 tablespoons RASPBERRY JELLY OR PRESERVES
4 RIPE PEACHES, PEELED, HALVED AND PITTED

Preheat the oven to 375°F. Put the rice, milk, 1 tablespoon of the sugar, and the nutmeg into a pan. Bring to a boil, then lower the heat and simmer very gently for about 25 minutes, stirring frequently, until the rice is cooked and most of the milk absorbed.

Beat the egg yolks into the rice, then pour into a 10-cup soufflé dish. Place a little raspberry jelly or preserve in each peach half. Arrange some of the peaches around the inside of the soufflé dish, with the cut sides pressing against the sides of the dish. Place the remaining peaches, jelly-side down, on the rice. Whisk the egg whites until stiff. Whisk in half the remaining sugar, then fold in the remainder. Spoon on top of the rice. Bake for about 5 minutes. Serve hot, or leave to cool then chill before serving. SERVES 8

LEFT: PEACH MERINGUE DESSERT
RIGHT: RASPBERRY BRÛLÉE

Calas Tous Chauds

Calas are rice fritters that were sold in the streets of the French Quarter in New Orleans by women known as Calas women. Their early morning cries of 'Calas Tous Chauds' would bring out the residents for their early morning snack. This recipe needs to be started a day in advance.

3/4 cup SHORT-GRAIN RICE

3 3/4 cups WATER

1/2 teaspoon SALT

1 PACKAGE DRY YEAST

1/2 cup WARM WATER

2 tablespoons SUGAR

3 LARGE EGGS

1 teaspoon GRATED LEMON ZEST

1/4 teaspoon GRATED NUTMEG

2 cups ALL-PURPOSE FLOUR

OIL FOR FRYING

POWDERED (CONFECTIONER'S) SUGAR

Sauce

3 tablespoons SOFT LIGHT BROWN SUGAR

2 tablespoons MAPLE SYRUP

2 teaspoons WATER

1 tablespoon UNSALTED BUTTER

1 tablespoon CHOPPED PECANS

Put the rice, water and salt into a saucepan. Bring to a boil. Cover and simmer for 30 minutes until the rice is very soft. Drain, cool, and mash the rice. Dissolve the yeast in the warm water with 1 teaspoon of the sugar, according to the instructions on the package. Pour the yeast liquid into the rice. Stir well. Cover with a damp linen cloth and leave in a warm place overnight.

The next day, beat the eggs with the remaining sugar, the lemon zest, nutmeg and two-thirds of the flour. Add to the rice mixture and beat well. Beat in the remaining flour for 2 minutes. Cover with a damp linen cloth and leave to rise in a warm place for 1 hour.

To make the sauce, put the sugar, maple syrup, water and butter into a small saucepan. Heat slowly, stirring until the sugar has dissolved. Stir in the pecans, cover, and keep warm over a very low heat. Pour a 1-inch layer of oil into a shallow skillet. Heat to 375°F using a thermometer. Preheat the oven to 375°F. Carefully spoon four portions of the rice mixture into the oil, and fry for 2 minutes, turning once. Check the temperature of the oil regularly. Drain on paper towels and keep warm in the oven while frying the rest. Dust the fritters with powdered sugar. Serve hot with the sauce. MAKES 24

Spicy Indian Rice Pudding

Long-grain rice can be substituted for basmati rice in this recipe.

4 CARDAMOM PODS

1 tablespoon BUTTER

1/2 cup BASMATI WHITE RICE

2 tablespoons SLIVERED ALMONDS

2 1/2 cups MILK

2 tablespoons SOFT BROWN SUGAR

Slit the cardamom pods open and remove the seeds. Crush the seeds with a rolling-pin. Melt the butter in a saucepan, add the crushed seeds and rice, and cook gently for 1 minute. Add the almonds and milk. Bring to a boil, cover, and simmer very gently for 20 minutes, stirring frequently, until the rice is tender and the liquid has been absorbed. Stir in the sugar and serve. SERVES 4

RIGHT: CALAS TOUS CHAUDS

R-Ice Coconut Cream

This is an unusual ice cream studded with the texture of rice which has absorbed the delicate fragrance of jasmine tea. You can substitute long-grain rice for jasmine rice in this recipe.

1 teaspoon	JASMINE TEA LEAVES
1/2 cup	BOILING WATER
1/4 cup	JASMINE RICE
2	EGGS
2 tablespoons	SUGAR
1 tablespoon	CORNSTARCH
1 1/4 cup	MILK
1/2 cup	CREAMED COCONUT, FINELY CHOPPED
1/2 cup	HEAVY CREAM

To Serve

2 tablespoons	DRIED COCONUT
	FRESH FRUIT SALAD
	JASMINE TEA

Put the tea leaves into a jug, and pour in the boiling water. Steep for 5 minutes. Strain the tea into a saucepan. Add the rice and cook as directed on page 14. Cool.

Whisk together the eggs, sugar and cornstarch. Heat the milk in a saucepan until almost boiling, then pour over the egg mixture, whisking continuously. Return to the pan and heat gently, stirring, until the mixture thickens. Do not boil. Remove from the heat and stir in the creamed coconut. Leave to cool.

Put the cold cooked rice and the cream into a food processor, blend until smooth, then stir into the cooled egg mixture. Pour into a 1-quart shallow freezer container and freeze for 2 hours. Cover and store.

To serve, remove from the freezer 1½ hours before required. Preheat the broiler. Toast the dried coconut until golden. Unmold the ice cream and cut into 6-8 portions. Sprinkle with the coconut. Serve with fresh fruit salad and jasmine tea.   SERVES 6-8

Chocolate Treats

4 squares	DARK CHOCOLATE, CHOPPED
4 squares	WHITE CHOCOLATE, CHOPPED
4 tablespoons	BUTTER OR MARGARINE, CHOPPED
2 tablespoons	MAPLE SYRUP
1 cup	RICE KRISPIES
2 tablespoons	CHOPPED CANDIED CHERRIES
1/2 cup	DARK CHOCOLATE CHIPS
1/2 cup	WHITE CHOCOLATE CHIPS

Melt the chocolate squares in two separate medium-sized bowls, placed over a pan of hot water. Melt the butter or margarine and maple syrup in a small saucepan, then pour half the mixture over the dark chocolate, the remainder over the white chocolate. Stir well, then stir in the Rice Krispies and cherries. Cool until just before setting, then stir the white chocolate chips into the dark chocolate mixture and the dark chocolate chips into the white chocolate mixture. Spoon into paper candy cups. Refrigerate to set.

MAKES APPROXIMATELY 30

TOP: CHOCOLATE TREATS   BOTTOM: R-ICE COCONUT CREAM

SPICY PLUM RICE PUDDINGS

2½ cups MILK
⅓ cup SHORT-GRAIN RICE
1 tablespoon SUGAR
½ teaspoon GROUND CINNAMON
2 LARGE EGGS, BEATEN
2-3 PLUMS, PITTED AND SLICED
3-4 teaspoons HONEY, WARMED

Preheat the oven to 325°F. Put the milk, rice, sugar and cinnamon into a saucepan. Bring to a boil, cover, and simmer gently for about 25 minutes, stirring occasionally. Cool slightly, then stir in the eggs.

Grease and line bases of a 6-8 cup muffin pan or use 2¼-inch-deep individual molds. Arrange some of the sliced plums in the base of each cup or mold, then spoon in the rice pudding, and stand in a roasting pan half-filled with hot water. Cover each cup or mold completely with oiled foil. Bake for 50 minutes. Remove from the roasting pan and leave for 10 minutes. Turn over onto small plates and spoon on the warm honey.

SERVES 6-8

LEMON RICE CARAMEL

⅔ cup SHORT-GRAIN RICE
3 cups MILK
½ cup HEAVY CREAM
3 EGGS, BEATEN
grated zest and juice of 1 LEMON

Caramel
1 cup SUGAR
6 tablespoons WATER

To make the caramel, put the sugar and water into a small saucepan and heat gently, until the sugar dissolves. Bring to a boil and boil gently, without stirring, until golden. Remove the pan from the heat and allow to darken a little more. Pour into eight 2½-inch-deep molds or cups, or into a 1-quart ring mold. Swirl the dishes so the sides are well coated. Set aside.

Preheat the oven to 325°F. Put the rice and milk into another saucepan. Bring to a boil, cover, and simmer very gently for 25 minutes. Cool slightly, then stir in the cream, eggs, lemon zest and juice. Spoon the rice mixture over the caramel and bake for 30 minutes for individual molds, 1 hour for a large mold, or until firm. Unmold onto small plates immediately. Serve hot or cold.

SERVES 8

LEFT: SPICY PLUM RICE PUDDING   RIGHT: LEMON RICE CARAMEL

INDEX

Acknowledgments

The authors and publisher would like to thank the following:
The US Rice Council, The UK Rice Association and Ente Nazionale Risi; Annabel Carmichael for typing
the original manuscript; and Lesley Scott for contributing some recipe material. Thanks also go to Debbie Boeger for
the California Company recipe and to Laverne Seidenstricker for the Camphouse Trout recipe.

Photography Credits

All photography is credited to Simon Butcher, except the following:
Clint Brown, pages 37 and 73; and Melvin Grey, page 81.